A *Must* Pre-Read:
Seven Essential Tips before You Read *Doubtbusters*

Doubtbusters! God Is My Shrink! is an important book to understand. Therefore, I, your author and narrator, prepared these essential tips to prepare you for this extraordinary journey. You will thank me afterwards, I hope!

The following seven bits of information are designed to help you, my soon-to-be-informed reader, pause briefly to understand my approach as the author of this book. It's also important for you to understand the book's character and characters and, thus, to appreciate how it's different as you read it. Also, my e-mail is doubtbusters7@gmail.com when you want to ask me questions or engage in a friendly discussion about the Subject of this book.

A book for doubters—everyone: You and I doubt God and his Bible. I can make that audacious statement because at any time in our lives that we fail to pray to God for his guidance, we doubt him. Any time we get frustrated or anxious, we doubt God. Also, when we let our circumstances determine our opinions and thoughts instead of God through prayer, we doubt his ability to guide us. Therefore, everyone needs this book, because we're all doubters at times.

The origin of the book's idea (the author as narrator and fictitious characters): The idea for writing this book came to me in the middle of one night in the summer of 2007, when I couldn't sleep. The concept entered my mind clearly but not audibly that I was to write a book about *why* Christians believe *what* they believe. Furthermore, my writing of the book was to include ongoing conversations and experiences—a journey—between the *real* me with my *genuine* experiences and a *fictional* man named Joe Smith with his *fictional* experiences and the fictional experiences we experience together. The idea was that specific!

The only true occurrence between Joe and me is the one in Part 15. God provided that same powerful action between me and a real 81-year-old friend named John; it really happened! Also, all of my testimonies to Joe about God's work in my life happened exactly the way I describe them.

The other main character in the book, Holly Holmes, arrived later in my writing and revising. She arrives on the journey in Part Three out of fifteen and gets the last word.

A nonfiction-fiction book: Your author completely concocted the rest of Joe's experiences. However, Joe Smith is very different from my real friend John in many other ways, except for the event during the turning point in Part 15 and the fact that John also rejected Christian beliefs until that climax. This book is nonfiction because of the non-fictional narrator's shared experiences, the final turning point, and the book's ideas, even though the plot and setting are almost completely fiction. It is all *so confusing*, as Joe might declare!

How the idea for the book grew: During the next few months, after that idea came to me, that concept that I believe came from God grew as I "bounced it off of" several people. It became a firm, full-blown idea that fall when I read in the Omaha newspaper—we lived in South Dakota near Nebraska at the time—that a Mormon leader defended the belief of Mitt Romney, then a presidential candidate, in the official Mormon belief that the three Persons of God are separate, not one God. More recently, an opinion poll came to my attention that a large percentage of Christian church leaders also believe that God is three separate Persons, not one God! In addition, another poll of Christians revealed that many of them do not know basic Christian beliefs.

Interestingly and sadly, many Mormons have discovered during their visits with professing Christians that many of them also believe that God is three separate Persons. Such reports confirmed for me the need to write this book to help Christians and non-Christians alike understand, as far as we can comprehend (which isn't very far), the amazing beliefs that the Bible presents about our awesome God, who is the *one*, only God in three Persons.

Steps in this book's model for personal relationship-building: At the same time you will see modeled throughout this book my approach of personal friendship toward all people. God has blessed in my real life that friendly way of developing relationships with unconditional love ("disagreeing agreeably," the way Joe and I put it), during which complete strangers have become my genuine friends, whether or not they became Christians. Even though that process takes patience, it is deeply rewarding. On some occasions people became God's friends as well. The steps of my personal-friendship approach, which you will see shown in the book, follow:

1. I break the barrier of silence by asking a question or making a friendly observation.
2. I discover a point of contact (something that the other person and I have in common).
3. I become an acquaintance with a growing, genuine friendship based on God's grace and love.
4. I share similar experiences, but also give God the credit in our conversations as I seek his blessings, while I persistently pray for God's filling and his words to speak.
5. I pray for the Holy Spirit's filling and guidance in the struggles of life.
6. I share the good news of Jesus in love at the right time on this friendly "journey."
7. I continue in friendship doing the things that friends do as I continue praying and sharing.
8. Hopefully, the non-Christian becomes a Christian, when our friendship becomes fellowship.
9. The other person attends a Bible-study group and a church, where the fellowship grows.

NOTE: A point of contact means that the other person has some quality or interest in common with you to which you can relate. For example, my real friend John had no interest in common with me, certainly not Christian beliefs. However, we both had a sense of humor which God used to keep our friendship going for three years. Also, he enjoyed talking about religion.

If you cannot find any point of contact at all either with your personalities or interests, invite them to your church and keep praying for them that God will send other Christians into their lives.

Informal but not too informal language: In addition, you will notice the occasional, informal language of *Doubtbusters*. It never involves crude or swearing words. That fact is also explained in the book. However, it does involve conversational words between Joe and the narrator with "g-dropping" in "-in**g**" words that don't have the accent on the "-ing" during a few times when we are kidding around. That informal language is a middle-class, especially-male, informal kind of speaking mostly when males are talking in less-than-serious ways as well as in certain dialects and areas of America.

Also, the conversations may seem a little artificial sometimes. That fact is because I've noticed that people speak a little more formally with me, a pastor, than they might otherwise.

The book's storyline that needs to be read straight through: My very important advice is that you read this book straight through instead of immediately going to the parts of the questions which interest you most. The reason is that this book has a storyline of a journey toward a goal as well as information. On the other hand, if you skip over the information for the story, you may miss reasons to be comforted by evidence for the Christian faith.

God's adopted child, Bruce Leiter.

Let *Doubtbusters! God Is My Shrink!* begin!

INSIDE *Doubtbusters! God Is My Shrink!*

The Writing of *Doubtbusters*: This nonfiction book contains the following two kinds of writing that flow together involving the fictional friendship of the real Christian author (as the narrator) and two fictional unbelievers Joe Smith and Holly Holmes, thus combining fiction and nonfiction:

I. **FICTION:** The events that the narrator, Holly, and Joe experience, their discussions, and their relationship are fictional in story form, except for Joe's experience at the end. The author deliberately chose to place apologetics and evangelism in a fictional framework because of the present-day interest in stories rather than propositional truth.

II. **NONFICTION:**

    A. The book will be classified as nonfiction because of the nonfictional narrator's reasons for Christian beliefs, including an unusual one that runs throughout the book.

    Furthermore, descriptions of the author-narrator's soap-opera Christian life in his testimonies to Joe and Holly all happened exactly the way they are described.

    In addition, Joe's amazing experience toward the end actually happened between the author and his unbelieving 81-year-old friend.

    B. The book also addresses the following questions in the fifteen parts of the book in order, as the narrator, Holly (beginning in Part 3), and Joe discuss Christian beliefs. The book tells a continuous story with nonfictional content:

    Part 1: What is God's relationship with the universe? 1. A hot-tub connection, 2. More discovery, 3. A revealing golf outing, 4. A challenging sports event, 5. A good but bad day, 6. A traumatic discovery.

Part 2: How does God reveal himself? 7. An anxious trip, 8. Hospital friendship, 9. Mysterious mathematics, 10. Good rehab torture, 11. Alarming news, 12. A very helpful group, 13. Amazing drama.

Part 3: How can we deal with our imperfections? 14. Imperfections, 15. More imperfections, 16. A "Routine" Morning Errand, 17. Help from above, 18. Debriefing.

Part 4: Why Is the Bible Important? 19. An important book, 20. A great book about a free gift, 21. Real permanent change, 22. A mysterious God revealed, 23. A mysterious disappearance, 24. Joe's revelation, 25. An explanation of evil.

Part 5: Who is Jesus? 26. A deep, dark secret, 27. A perfect Father, 28. Real peace, 29. Coping with pain.

Part 6: What is God like? 30. An arrest, 31. A bleak visit, 32. Miracles? 33. Human assumptions.

Part 7: What will happen to us after we die? 34. Surprising diagnosis, 35. New bodies.

Part 8: How many ways are there to God? 36. A new heart, 37. No excuses, 38. Comedy, 39. Real prayer, 40. An uncomfortable trial.

Part 9: What is Jesus going to do in the future? 41. Justice, 42. A future event, 43. A sad announcement, 44. God's golf course, 45. Sheep or goats?

Part 10: Does God punish humans? 46. Robots and humans, 47. An amazing rescue, 48. A hot-tub arrival, 49. Successful surgery, 50. Getting acquainted.

Part 11: How important is the church? 51. New attenders, 52. What's the point? 53. Imperfect people, 54. A vision, 55. Fellowship.

Part 12: How can God love us? 56. Loving and forgiving? 57. Unconditional love, 58. The source of human talent.

Part 13: What do believers have to do with Abraham? 59. New things, 60. Abraham, where are you? 61. Free love, 62. Little differences.

Part 14: How do divine and human plans work together? 63. Sad Story, 64. Helpful discussion, 65. Late golf.

Part 15: How does God overcome doubt permanently? 66. Baptism, 67. Fervent prayer, 68. First visit, 69. An amazing visit, 70. An exciting visit, 71. A tragic triumph.

© 2011 Bruce Leiter
All Rights Reserved.

No part of this publication may be reproduced, stored in a retrieval system, or transmitted, in any form or by any means, electronic, mechanical, photocopying, recording, or otherwise, without the written permission of the author.

First published by Dog Ear Publishing
4010 W. 86th Street, Ste H
Indianapolis, IN 46268
www.dogearpublishing.net

ISBN: 978-1-4575-0795-3

This book is printed on acid-free paper.

Printed in the United States of America

ACKNOWLEDGEMENTS

I acknowledge the support and help of my wonderful wife, Winnie; my writers' group, Word Weavers of West Michigan; editors and readers; Pastor Brian Bosscher; Professor Quentin Schultz of Calvin College, at whose workshop the title was born; and all who gave me feedback about the book. My thanks go to all of you whom God used to shape it. Ultimately, the honor goes to the 3-in-1 God of the Bible, who gave me the idea for *Doubtbusters* and guided its writing and revising. Bruce Leiter the Writer.

Doubtbusters!
God Is My Shrink!

by Bruce Leiter

PART 1

How is God Related to the Universe?

CHAPTER 1

A hot-tub connection

As I swam my many laborious but helpful laps at the small-town, indoor swimming pool, the only other swimmer in the pool, a stranger to me, abruptly ended his swim and ambled toward the hot-tub.

The late-afternoon sun glistened like a thousand golden jewels on the almost-deserted pool. I ended my thirty-minute swim and lowered my body into the 103-degree hot-tub water—ah, dessert after the main meal!

That other occupant of the hot-tub was a heavy-set, thirty-something man, who was bent over as if he carried the weight of the universe on his shoulders, Atlas-like. Following my usual custom, I broke the American "wall of silence" with a loud whisper, "Hi, how are you doing today?"

Without making eye contact, he responded so softly that I could hardly hear him six feet away in the opposite corner of the spa, "O...K...."

"I don't believe that we've met. I'm Bruce Leiter."

He mumbled while staring at the hot-tub bubbles, "I'm Joe—Joe Smith."

"You're Joe Smith, the pro-basketball player? You don't look like him!"

After Joe paused, his answer came with a beginning gleam in his eye. For the first time his eyes met my friendly, half-smiling gaze, "No, I'm a slightly-different color...and a little-bit shorter," he replied with a tiny grin on his oval face, while gradually raising and holding the index finger and thumb on his right hand as close together as he could without touching them. He straightened his body in response to my natural friendliness like a robin emerging from its shell.

We chortled at his cleverness. This heavy-set man reminded me a little bit of the hunchback of Notre Dame as we shook hands, his hand feeling like a limp locker-room towel in mine. He continued, "I'm not...the NBA player, but I...have become a Chicago Bulls fan since he joined them last year, even though he was then traded to the Cleveland Cavaliers."

"Do you know, Joe, that the Cleveland *Indians* have a right-handed, side-armed relief pitcher also named Joe Smith?"

"I guess...I do...now."

I continued with growing warmth toward this solemn, gentle, seemingly-broken young man, "Your basketball namesake sure has a smooth jump-shot. I've been a Bulls fan since they started playing back in 1966. That same winter my wife, Winnie, and I watched them play Wilt Chamberlain and the 76ers when we lived in Evergreen Park near Chicago. That year the Bulls had the best expansion-team record ever. Do you know why they're called the Bulls?"

Joe's muscles relaxed a little, "No..., I don't."

"Well, we watched them play in the old Amphitheater next to the old stockyards, both of which are now history...."

He jumped in with a half-smile, "...and...that's why they were called the Bulls..., like their 'ex-neighbors'?"

"Yeah, I think so. So, Joe, how is it that I've never seen you at this Iowa small-town pool before?"

Joe's tongue suddenly loosened up, "Well, I moved here recently after my wife died, when I got a job in the Quad-Cities as a computer analyst. Because I didn't want to live in the city, I found a nice house here only a forty-minute drive from work. However, now I'm between jobs and have moved back in with my parents, who also live here in town," as he again studied the ripples of the spa.

I lowered my voice, "May I ask what happened to your wife?"

I could see tears in the corners of his eyes as he answered, "She had cancer. I kept telling her to get it checked out, but you know how people can be...," as his voice trailed off, while he leaned back and stared at the rafters. We sat in the hot-tub for what seemed like an hour until I quietly broke the silence, "That's horrible, Joe! She was way too young to die."

Eventually, after a long pause, Joe regained his natural grin and mustered his curiosity enough to ask, "What do you do for a living?"

"I'm a retired preacher. My wife and I moved here recently after our retirement."

"A retired preacher *and* a sports fan—an interesting combination!" Joe's body then floated toward me, attached with his arms to the northeast corner of the hot-tub.

I sat up on the edge of the hot-tub so that I wouldn't get dizzy from the hot water as I replied with a smile while counting "six" on my fingers, "O, I limit my sports-watching to *only* six sports (a person has to limit himself!): baseball, basketball, football, tennis, golf. I count the Olympics as my sixth one!" Joe grinned his first full grin.

I swept my arm toward the pool, "May I ask what you do to relax, besides swimming?"

"I enjoy watching football, baseball, an occasional movie, and basketball as well as playing golf once in a while."

"I used to golf, as more of a duffer than a golfer, but I quit because my back was acting up. I gave my rusty golf clubs, which I bought at a garage sale for twenty bucks, to my oldest son. However, he stopped using them and returned them to me. My back's better, probably because of this relaxing place. As a result, I thought that I might start golfing again."

"I do it for fun and relaxation."

"Me, too! Maybe we can go golfing some time."

"Yeah, that's a great idea!"

CHAPTER 2

More discovery

The next day I arrived at the swimming pool about fifteen minutes later than the previous day. Joe was already in the water. He waved to me with a grin as he made a turn and as I inched into the 80-degree water for my on-my-back-with-arms-under-the-water swim. When I finished, Joe was already basking in the soothing heat of the social spa.

I asked as I leaned forward, "How are you...doing today, Joe?"

"OK. Say, Bruce, I want to apologize for yesterday."

"Think nothing of it, Joe. There's nothing to apologize for. We all have things to grieve about. Back in 1972 my wife and I lost our second boy, Keith, due to leukemia. He was sick almost three years, a very traumatic time in our lives when we both came down with hepatitis. But God was with us. After I wept a little at Keith's bedside, I went back to work as a junior-high teacher, thinking that I was over it...."

"At this point in my life, I don't even know if God *exists*."

After a pause I empathized, "I can understand your feelings after what you have experienced, Joe. I'm a little curious about what you said yesterday. How...did you lose...your job?"

He summed up his feelings in one angry, loud word that drew a look from the lanky, young male lifeguard, "*Downsizing*!"

I protested with wrinkled eyebrows and a clenched fist, "Yeah, companies almost always think more about profits than people nowadays!" A long empathetic silence followed.

Regaining his composure, Joe cut the silence as with a cleaver, "What baseball team do you follow?"

"I grew up on a small farm near Gurnee, Illinois, north of Chicago, watching and rooting for the Cubs after Dad brought home our first TV in 1951, when TVs were getting popular. I was a nine-year-old boy bored with farm work. As a result, TV and sports became my escape from what I considered to be the drudgery of the farm. How about you?"

"Well, I grew up on the south side of Chicago in the Roseland area. Unlike the rest of my family, who were Sox fans, I watched and rooted for the Cubs. I've stuck with them ever since then. However, we moved here before I began ninth grade."

"Amazing! Here, I meet another loyal Cub fan at an Iowa indoor pool not far from the Quad-Cities! You know, of course, that the Cubs are going to win it all in this year, 2008, the hundred-year anniversary of their last World-Series win!" Our high-five splashed water in all directions.

"Yes, they are!" We again splashed a boisterous high-five.

After a pause, while leaning forward and making full eye-contact, I asked, "Say, Joe, now that it's already the middle of May with much of spring behind us, let's go golfing."

"Let's do that. How's this coming Saturday afternoon for you?"

I responded with a nasal voice, while hesitating with a smile; holding up my empty, wet hands to page through my imagined calendar; and ending my response with my usual mid-range voice, "Well,...I'll have to check...my retirement...calendar,...but it sounds like fun!" We laughed with the sounds of our new-found friendship.

CHAPTER 3

A revealing golf outing

    That Saturday afternoon was perfect for golf with the temperature in the mid-70s, a deep-blue Iowa sky, and a few fleecy clouds floating overhead. I picked Joe up at his parents' house in my Pontiac Vibe. Then, we traveled east forty minutes to a nine-hole public golf course, a hilly stretch of land straddling a tributary emptying into the Mississippi River. I had never played there. However, it offered half-price greens fees for ministers and their guests.

    I smirked as I surveyed the hilly and watery scene, "O, good! Now, we can battle the water, sand, *and* trees! My golf balls have 'magnets' that attract them to all three. This course looks as if it has an abundance of that dreaded threesome! However, the pinches of Dutch and Scottish in me both appreciate the half-price cost for ministers."

    Joe remarked just before he teed off on the first hole, "All you have to do is concentrate, concentrate, concentrate!"

    He was 5'10" with a heavy build, but his drive whistled 300 yards down the first fairway like a Canada goose flying straight south to its winter destination. However, my 6'4" 250-pound frame could only muster 225 yards off into the right-hand rough, a fairly lengthy drive for my game. My eyes and mouth opened wide. "How do you do that?"

    Joe winked as we walked to our balls, "There are ten movements of the human body that need to be coordinated to make a good golf swing. I should have added earlier to my comment about concentrating, 'All you have to do is coordinate, coordinate, coordinate!'"

    I raised my voice as I headed into the rough, "Now I know why I've never been very good at golf. I've never been very coordinated. Of course, there's an advantage to slicin' and hookin' the ball instead of hittin' it straight."

Smiling Joe yelled to me from the fairway, "What's that?"

"I get more exercise zigzaggin' up and down the course," as I made a snake-like motion with my hand. He grinned as I chopped out of the rough in the direction of the green. "Well, amazin'!" I said with a big grin, as my ball laid up a few yards from the cup in the rough on the right side of the green.

Then Joe landed his second shot with only one brief bounce ten feet from the pin, while my chip shot sailed into the sand bunker to the left of the green. My next shot ended up a few inches from the hole, while Joe slid his putt into the cup. "Great shot, Joe!" I shouted as we high-fived.

Thus, the afternoon went by quickly with Joe's par-bogey golf (very good, non-professional golf) and my bogey-double-bogey-triple-bogey golf (average, occasional golf).

Finally, we trudged to the highest point of the course, the ninth tee. We emerged on a narrow path through a row of ten-foot-high, sweet-smelling, pale-yellow Primerose lilac bushes on the west side of the eighth green. Suddenly, a panorama of the Mississippi River Valley spread out before us. The course's veranda clubhouse below us was 610 yards away. A meandering stream cut the fairway in three parts. Checkered farmfields lay on the horizon beyond the wide river.

With a wide sweep of my arms, I exclaimed, "What a beautiful creation God made!"

Joe's face had a full frown, "How can you believe that God made all of that? I believe that it only happened because of natural processes!"

"Maybe, but I believe that God spoke it into being or used natural processes to make all of it—or both! Either way, he did it. That's what I believe!" I riveted my gaze on the scene, raised my arms toward the heavens, and pointed them at the horizon, "That's what it says in God's Word, the Bible, 'In the beginning God created the heaven and the earth.' Consider the amazing variety and similar design in the universe, like the design of the atom and the solar system. Electrons and planets all revolve around their centers! Also, we are experiencing today, Joe, God's faithful changing of the seasons. How can you *not* believe in a divine Designer with that fantastic scene in front of you?"

"I understand your point, but how can you believe that a book full of fantastic fairy tales is God's Word?" He teed off with a straight-arrow shot halfway to the ninth-green target.

As we walked together to my shorter ball, which landed gently on the lush green fairway this time, I rejoined, "I believe that God revealed himself in the Bible because at that time the idea that there was a separate Creator of everything was a brand-new, revolutionary thought. No one believed that idea in the ancient world, since all of the 'gods' of that time were thought to be *parts* of creation. The people of that time worshiped the sun, moon, sea, earth, and sky. Human reasoning can come up with the idea that all visible things are gods, because we can see them.

"However, along came Moses with a new, completely different, invisible God, separate from his creation but very much involved in it. Such a God no one could have ever imagined! After all, how can you doubt that an amazingly-designed, complex universe, part of which we have experienced this afternoon, has a divine Designer?"

Joe's silence that lasted on our whole walk to the green showed me that he had never seriously considered such ideas. As I tapped my ball into the cup on the ninth hole for my first par of the afternoon, I said, "I had a great time, Joe! You played great!"

"You didn't do so bad yourself, Bruce, especially on that last hole."

"Hey, Joe, the Cubs are on TV next Tuesday night. Why don't we watch them together at my house."

Joe drawled with a big grin, "OK, p-a-rd-ner!"

* * *

"To whom will you compare me? Or who is my equal?" says the Holy One. "Lift up your eyes and look to the heavens: Who created all these? He who brings out the starry host one by one and calls them each by name. Because of his great power and mighty strength, not one of them is missing"

(Isaiah 40:25,26).

* * *

CHAPTER 4

A challenging sports event

The following Tuesday night in my surround-sound room with a 50-inch TV, we rooted the Cubs on, until Derrick Lee slammed a three-run, walk-off homer deep into the left-field bleachers to win the game in the bottom of the ninth inning. After Joe and I high-fived the Cubs' win, I said, "The Cubs certainly have a lot of God-given talent that they're using well this year."

Sitting on the blue well-stuffed couch to the right of my recliner but without meeting my gaze, Joe crossed his arms, put his right leg on the couch, and retorted, "You mean that their use of their talent isn't to their credit!?"

I replied to Joe's doubt, "Sure, they're using their talent, but I believe that God is its original Source and Enabler, since I believe that God made every human body and gives us strength for each day. Just like your ability to golf on Saturday, I believe that the ultimate credit for baseball and golf abilities goes to God, who made us and reveals himself in his creation. That's what his Word, which also reveals him from cover to cover, says."

My wife, Winnie, invaded my "man-cave" through the door to the left of the TV leading upstairs and interrupted our discussion with the offer of some soda and brownies. After she left, Joe waded with me into the deep, treacherous waters of discussion about God, "Bruce, you talk about the Bible as if God told the writers what to write."

I was willing to swim in that water with him without drowning, "Yeah, I've read through the Bible several times. Each time I have become more and more convinced that God led the prophets and apostles to write those words because God himself is an amazing, mysterious God. Joe, no one can ever imagine a personal God who is completely separate from the universe. Also, we can't imagine that he is completely involved in all of the details of his creation at the same time and that he is all-powerful, all-knowing, everywhere-present, and has always existed. No one could have dreamed up the Bible's God!"

After Joe's silence, I continued, "You said Saturday that you thought that the Bible is 'full of fantastic fairy tales.' May I ask what you meant by that statement?"

Joe rested his chin on his hand, "Well, it seems to me that since I can't see God, how can I believe in him, especially the many unusual things said about him in that book?"

"Well, do you believe in the wind that moved our golf balls around on Saturday and that blows home runs out of Wrigley Field about half of the time?"

"Of course, I do!" Joe smirked.

"But you can't *see* the wind. How can you *believe* in it?" I replied with a matching smirk.

"I see what you mean. I can believe in the wind because of what it does. You're saying that the God of the Bible can be believed because of the design and regular events that show his power in the world around us?"

"Yeah, you got it!"

"But what about the stories like David, a mere boy, killing a nine-foot giant and Jesus walking on water? Those stories were only a couple of the unbelievable stories that I heard in Sunday School?"

"Is it so unbelievable that a God who made and guides all things, as he is revealed so clearly in the Bible, could give such abilities to people? It's not at all unbelievable when it involves Jesus, who claimed to be God! Are those stories beyond the realm of possibility if you grant that God made the human body and the earth?"

"Well, I'm still not convinced!"

"Joe, when was the last time you read the Bible?"

"I've never read it all the way through. I have this old Bible that my grandma gave me when I was a boy."

I got up, retrieved a dark-blue Bible from my downstairs writing desk in the same room, and said, "Here, this is the *New International Version*, which was translated directly from the original languages in everyday words. You can have this one, which won't have the language barrier of the older version. I invite you to prove to yourself whether God inspired it or not. It's my belief that, because the God that's presented there from beginning to end, is beyond human thinking, he must have revealed himself to those writers and, therefore, to us."

"I'll take you up on your challenge. I've been looking for a book to read, but I'm not going to be easy to convince."

"Fair enough, Joe. I hope that we can *agree to disagree* about God and the Bible, while still remaining friends."

"How can we not as loyal Cub fans?!" he agreed with a laugh.

CHAPTER 5

A bad but good day

When I entered the men's locker room, I spied Joe. I could tell by his glum look that he was having a bad day. He looked like an orangutan that went without his supper—minus all the hair, of course. I inquired, "How...are you doing,...Joe?"

His locker, where he always dressed, was actually a half-locker along the wall on the right side behind a wall near the entrance. Mine was half-way down the left side of the sweat-smelling room.

He responded with descending inflection, "Pretty good."

"What do you mean by 'pretty good'?" I inquired as I inched toward him.

"Well, I've been having a bad day 'cause today would have been Jean's birthday. She always enjoyed getting something from me, no matter what it was...." His voice trailed off.

"Tell me about her." I sat down on his bench.

After a long pause, Joe looked at me with tears tracing down his face, "She was pretty and a lot of fun. Her sense of humor was second to none."

"Her absense is a big hole in your life, isn't it, Joe?"

He nodded silently, as tears rimmed his blood-shot eyes.

In the hot-tub forty minutes later, we were all alone again when Joe surprised me with an unexpected question as he met my friendly gaze, "Bruce, how old was your boy when he died?"

"Four and a half, Joe. Keith was a real trooper inspite of all the spinal taps. His smile lit up the children's playroom at the University of Wisconsin Children's Hospital. He had all the nurses tied around his little finger. His personality was amazing. One time when we were camping, our oldest boy, Jim, characteristically brought a new-found friend back to our tent at the campground. He commented—as kids will—to Keith that he was really fat. A twinkle began in Keith's eyes as he stuck his stomach out as far as it would go and said, 'Do you want to see me *really* fat?'"

Joe managed a half-grin, "How could you go through losing your son?"

"Only with God, Joe, only with God. A week after we brought Keith home from the hospital, after we first learned that he had leukemia, Keith and Winnie were up all night with Keith's fever, which inched up to 105 degrees. It had snowed a couple of inches that cold Wisconsin February night when Winnie called Keith's doctor in Madison, a two-hour drive away at normal speed. The doctor—a caring, committed cancer physician—told her that we should take Keith to the UW Children's Hospital.

"As I drove carefully 45-miles-an-hour on the snow-covered Interstate to Madison, I eased the accelerator toward the floor to see if I could go faster but couldn't. A Cadillac hurtled past us but careened recklessly off into the right-hand ditch with its tail lights pointing upward at an odd angle. Winnie prayed that Keith wouldn't die in her arms and that God would give her his peace and assurance that he was with us even then, as Keith lay feverishly limp in her arms. I was praying desperately that God would rescue Keith.

"We finally arrived at the hospital, and our doctor stayed with Keith all of that day on his day off! We telephoned Kenosha that morning to ask the church to pray for Keith. About noon our doctor ushered us into a spare room to tell us that Keith had a 50%-50% chance to live. A strep infection was threatening his life because the immature leukemia white cells were a majority of the cells in his immune system. As a result, he had very little resistance to strep. Inspite of the odds against Keith, I sensed that God was with him and us!

"Winnie reported that when the doctor announced the seriousness of Keith's situation, God surprisingly created his peaceful assurance within her, thus revealing himself to her inspite of our dire circumstances.

"However, it wasn't until almost fifteen years later that God created in me that same kind of peace. It is a permanent peace that enables believers to stop being angry or anxious about a traumatic time in their lives. That peace from God enables believers to submit to tough times as parts of God's permissive plan for the improvement of their lives. We are both very thankful that God revealed himself to us in the middle of our suffering.

"It's because of that peace that is beyond human understanding, described by Paul in Philippians chapter four and given to both of us, that I know that the Bible is God's Book, where he's revealed. I believe that humans apart from God can't develop such a permanent peace, because human peace is based on circumstances. God's peace, on the other hand, is *inspite of* circumstances. Thus, the Bible must've come from that same God of permanent peace!

"Well, God answered all of our prayers, brought Keith through that life-threatening experience, and gave us two and a half more years with him. Winnie and I both felt much closer to God because of that experience, though it was *very* traumatic!"

Joe, who had been staring intently at me, exclaimed, "What an unlucky time you had!"

I answered with God's help, "Joe, I don't believe in luck. Instead, I believe that God allowed Keith's sickness and death to bring us closer to him. For example, Keith had leg problems at the same time. It was really God's gift of Keith's simple faith that the Lord used to help us. One day Keith was playing with his toys in the kitchen when he asked Winnie, 'Mom, will there be toys in heaven?'

"She said with God's leading, 'I don't know; the Bible doesn't say. But it does say that we will be very happy. If we will need toys to make us happy, God will provide them. However, I'm sure that there will be much better things to keep us happy.'

"Well, Keith couldn't imagine heaven without toys. However, he did say, 'My leg won't hurt there, will it, Mom?' Winnie could heartily agree with him, '…because the Bible says that there will be no more pain!'"

Joe lowered his stare to the steaming water, "I don't think that there's anything beyond death."

"I'm sure that there's a heaven, Joe, because the Bible says so. And I believe that God inspired that book to reveal himself, because much of what it says is beyond human imagination. It has to be from God because it says that he is an invisible Creator revealing himself in the Bible and in his creation."

"I began reading the Bible you gave me. What I can't understand is, how could all of the creation have happened in six days? I believe that it all came into being during billions of years by chance."

I responded, "Whether it happened in shorter or longer time—two ideas on which Christians need to agree to disagree—Moses said that the one true God, the Creator, did it all.

"The twenty-four-hour theory concerning each day's length believed by some Christians has support from the fact that the text says, 'the evening and the morning' of each day. Certainly, the all-powerful God could have made everything in six days while giving his handiwork the appearance of millions of years of time. After all, he is the Source and Ruler of the universe! He can do anything he wants to do.

"But it surely may have taken a much longer time. After all, the sun didn't get created until the fourth day. As a result, a twenty-four-hour day wasn't *possible* without a sun during the first three days and part of the fourth one. Also, the word *day* in the Bible is often used to mean a longer period of time. Furthermore, you did read in Genesis chapter one that God commanded the earth to 'bring forth' created things, which is language that seems to suggest a much longer time. Therefore, the Bible itself allows for both interpretations by believers."

"But I thought that it all began with a big bang."

"Well, neither the scientists nor we were there when it happened. The big bang and other scientific ideas about the universe's origins and diversity are all a matter of scientific theory that no one can ever prove as a fact, since no one wrote down their observations at the beginning of those eons for us to learn what really happened. God could have used a big bang or some other means.

"However, the Bible does clearly reveal the truth that a separate, invisible God, the one true God, not the gods then or now, created everything by the divine power of his Word. Virtually all professing Christians believe the revealed truth that the universe couldn't have come by chance but only from its Creator, no matter how he created it."

Undeterred by my answer, Joe pressed me further, "Contrary to the Genesis account, I believe that humans came from an ancestor that we had in common with the apes. After all, I've heard that we have 97% of our DNA in common with them!"

My response made Joe sit up straight, "Yes, we have similar structures like tailbones—I prefer the technical word 'coccyx'—and similar DNA. On the other hand, I believe that those similarities point, instead, to our mutual divine Designer.

"Joe, we also have 95% of our DNA similar to rats. I don't think that any scientist seriously states that humans descended from a common ancestor of rats! It's much easier for me to believe that a divine

Designer made everything in the light of such amazing designs as DNA than many people's conclusion that it all came by random combinations. To my thinking, that idea's the one that's unbelievable!"

Joe leaned forward, "How could a snake speak to tempt Eve into disobeying God's command not to eat the fruit in Eden?"

We rose to get our pre-swim shower, "Satan, a fallen angel whose rebellion against God is the source of all evil in the world, used the snake to deceive her with half-truths and downright lies. She and Adam thought that they knew better than God how to live their lives. The result has been that the human race has followed their lead in rebellion! The whole story is so much like human beings' turning their backs on their Creator. They've been playing the 'blame-game' like our first parents ever since!"

Joe quickly launched another dart toward me as his theological dartboard, "Do you think that I'm doing that?!"

I deftly deflected his dart back to him, "That's for you to determine. That's exactly what I did for the first sixteen years of my life by ignoring God. Because my mom expected me to attend church, I went through all of the God-motions of going to church, while secretly wishing that I was home with Dad. I even sang hymns that I didn't believe in the junior choir, from which I gladly excused myself when my voice changed."

Joe smirked at my passive-aggressive rebellion. I guessed that he had also rebelled similarly and continued, "I remember coming home from summer Bible camp one time really excited about the God of creation. But that emotional high wore off, since my life had not changed.

"However, after we switched churches when I was sixteen years old, God grabbed hold of me and permanently changed my life at the new church, where the preacher preached the God of the Bible. The results of God's revelation of himself and revolution in my life were that I then eagerly *wanted* to go to church to learn more about God and that I *wanted* to help my mother in the garden. I had previously *hated* both activities. God is still revealing his Word to me as I read the Bible!"

"Wow, you sure have had interesting experiences!"

"Joe, I believe that humans live daily in their natural, rebellious self-centeredness that God reveals honestly in the Bible. Since God is very different from our normal experience as the invisible, one true Creator and Rescuer, he *had* to have inspired that Book. Natural humans never could have imagined him, because he is very different from us in our post-Adam situation."

Joe's long, answering silence engulfed us as we headed for the pool. Perhaps, he was beginning to consider my ideas.

CHAPTER 6

A traumatic discovery

After my exercise skimming the surface that Friday, Winnie and I spent a week and a half at our friends' cottage in the Wisconsin North Woods, where no one knew our phone number. We returned refreshed, yet exhausted, on Monday ten days later. I went to the pool expecting to see Joe, but he wasn't there. His absence was so unlike him that I called his parents from my car.

Joe's younger sister, Phyllis, answered the telephone with a loud shriek, "Haven't you heard, Bruce!? I thought everyone in town had heard that Joe was in a horrible car accident this past Saturday! He was crossing Main Street in his Ford Festiva with the green light when a semi coming from the north ran the red light and slammed into Joe on the driver's side! At the same time, a car coming behind Joe on green crashed into the rear of Joe's car! Because he couldn't move his limbs, after they used the jaws of life to get him out of that tiny tin-can of a car, they rushed him by helicopter to the trauma center at Genesis Medical Center, East Campus, in Davenport. He's still in Intensive Care!"

* * *

> In the beginning was the Word, and the Word was with God, and the Word was God....Through him all things were made; without him nothing was made....The Word was made flesh and made his dwelling among us. We have seen his glory, the glory of the one and only Son, who came from the Father, full of grace and truth.
>
> (John 1:1,2,14)

Part One Discussion Questions

1. How does the narrator enable Joe Smith to "come out of his shell"? How can we "break the ice" in meeting and making acquaintances with new people whenever God puts them near us? Why would we want to make friends of strangers?

2. The narrator's response to Joe's expressed agnosticism (saying that he didn't know if God exists) was empathetic understanding. What other responses would have built bridges from the narrator to Joe? What responses would have built a wall between them? How would you have responded to Joe's unbelief? Why?

3. How did the narrator find points of contact between himself and Joe? How have you befriended strangers or acquaintances that God put near you—in your neighborhood, exercise place, or at work? How can we find ways to make similar points of contact with strangers who might become our friends? If we can't find any points of contact with them, what can we say or do anyway?

4. How did the narrator take advantage of the view from the ninth tee to express his faith? How can we gain the courage and words to share our beliefs in God?

5. How can we express our faith without building walls between us and other people?
What can we learn about building bridges instead of walls with other people from Part One?

6. When Joe said that he thought that the Bible was "full of fantastic fairy tales," what was your inner response? How would you have responded to that and other comments with which you disagree? What is the best way to respond? Why?

PART 2

How Does God Reveal Himself?

CHAPTER 7

An Anxious Trip

"That's horrible,...shocking news,...Phyllis!" I exclaimed, after a pause. Then I blurted, "I'm going right now to see him in Davenport!" A quick call to Winnie—to let her know where I was—began a forty-five-minute drive to Genesis Medical Center, East Rusholme Street Campus, in Davenport. During my quick trip, my head whirled with bits of shocked sentences, some trivial, others profound:

"...Why did this accident happen, God...?"

"...I've often heard that bad things happen in threes...."

"...Dear God, take care of Joe...!"

"...Why would Philip and Josephine name their children Phyllis and Joseph...?"

"...Why would you, Father, let this terrible thing happen to Joe when we've just met...?"

I sailed along I-80 with little traffic on that Monday afternoon. However, my usual decision to take expressways as much as possible backfired. When I exited on I-74 to go south, there was stop-and-start, caterpillar-crawling traffic for several blocks from I-80 to Middle Road. An accident that was, by now, off on the right side of the southbound lanes had caused what they call in Chicago a "gaper's block" that whole stretch.

"Human curiosity!!" I grumbled, spitting out those words as my Vibe crept impatiently past the accident. I finally exited, relieved, to go west on East Locust Street. I prayed, "Lord, forgive me for my impatience and make me more patient." Then I wondered aloud as I stared at the street signs, "Why would they name a street after an insect pest?" and laughed at my many unanswerable questions.

CHAPTER 8

Hospital Friendship

Suddenly, the word "Genesis" pierced my consciousness and caused a grin to creep across my face. I saw the medical center looming ominously with three rectangular window-eyes like some outer-space monster peering down on East Rusholme Street ready to gobble people up. "It's ironic, dear Lord, that Joe and I have been discussing you as the Creator, while at the same time he was taken to Genesis! Father, give him and his family—and me—strength. Give me your words through Jesus by your Spirit as I visit with Joe!" At that moment, I nudged my Vibe wagon into the hospital parking lot.

Visitors can only visit patients a few minutes every hour in the medical intensive-care unit. As I inquired at the nurses' station for his room number, out of the corner of my eye I suddenly glimpsed Joe. With all his bandages he looked a little like the Stay Puft Marshmellow Man in the Bill Murray and Dan Ackroyd 1984 flick *Ghostbusters*. As I tiptoed like a clumsy ballet dancer minus tights into Joe's room, I thought, *At least, he didn't experience the same final result that the Marshmellow Man did!* and whispered in his ear, "Hi, Joe."

He slowly opened his black-and-blue eyes and managed a partial smile, "Bruce, I'm glad...to see ya! They tell me...that I was in an accident."

"Yeah, your sister told me about it this afternoon when I missed you at the pool."

Joe winced as he took a painful breath and mustered the unanswerable question, "Bruce, how could *your* God allow this to happen to *me*,...if he *is* God?"

"O, Joe," I managed with a tear creeping down my left cheek, "I don't know. I asked him that question often as I drove here, but no answer came."

"They also tell me that my car became the filling of a semi-sedan sandwich and that I should be dead."

"I'm sure glad that God spared your life and rescued you, Joe!"

Undeterred, Joe rambled on with random thoughts, "But get this, Bruce, just about every bone in my body except for one was either bruised or broken,...and that lone bone is the coccyx, the tailbone!...A doctor once told me that swimming exercises every muscle in the body except one, the coccyx muscle!...I know how you feel about the use of the term 'tailbone.'...Not only that, but they took me to Genesis, Bruce!" he confided with a slow wink in his mock spy voice.

Just then, I noticed the dark-blue Bible that I had given him on his nightstand. I returned his reference to Genesis with a nod, "Yeah, that irony didn't escape me either. Do you want me to read the Bible or pray with you, Joe?"

A nurse entered Joe's room, ending our brief exchange. "That's OK, Bruce. I don't see how that would help."

I retreated between the glass doors, "I'll be back in an hour, Joe."

I ate a quick supper in the cafeteria and endured a slow, impatient eternity of vacant magazine reading. Finally, my turn with Joe arrived. Joe was ready for me with a surprising question, "Bruce, how can God be three but also one, the way they taught me in Sunday School?"

I briefly gathered my wits with a quick, unspoken prayer before my response, "Well, Joe, you have read in Genesis chapter one...that God said, 'Let *us* make human beings in *our* image, in *our* likeness,'...an Old Testament hint at his threeness....'

Then, I managed to explain further in choppy prose, "You will also read in Deuteronomy chapter six Moses' statement that '...the LORD our God, the LORD, is *one*,' as inspired Moses emphasized God's *oneness* in contrast to the many gods of all the other nations....In addition, John wrote at the beginning of his gospel, 'In the beginning was the Word, and the Word was *with* God, and the Word *was* God....Through him all things were made....The Word became flesh and made his dwelling among us.'

"...As a result, the Word *as God* but also *with God* the Father, of course, became Jesus, emphasizing both God's oneness *and* twoness....Later in John's gospel, in chapters fourteen, fifteen, and sixteen, Jesus predicts the coming of *another* Counselor, the Holy Spirit, who is believers' Lawyer-Friend. Those Bible references and several others are the reasons that Christians believe that God is three Persons—Father, Jesus, and Holy Spirit—in *one* God, *not three* Gods."

"But that idea doesn't make sense!" Joe protested.

I sat down on a folding chair, "Joe, there are many other gods in which humans believe. For example, the gods of many Native Americans, Hindus, Buddhists, New Agers, and the Force of *Star Wars'* fame are the *same* as the universe and the sum total of all things, including the human race. Also, the gods of Jehovah's Witnesses and Jews are *separate* from the universe but only one person. Furthermore, the god of the Mormons is three gods. In addition, a number of Muslim thinkers say that their Allah isn't a person, because that description would compare Allah to humans. Instead, many Muslims believe that Allah is the impersonal, unmoved Mover of the universe.

"Humans could've thought up all of those gods as alternate gods to the true God. But the mysterious-yet-revealed, three-Persons-in-one God of the Bible couldn't have been the product of any human minds.

"I've even met three people who believe that the true God is a generic god in whom all religions believe. That idea can't be true because the gods of the religions that I just mentioned are *very* different from each other."

"I see your point, but why do ya suppose there are so many gods?"

"It goes back to the Garden of Eden that you read about in Genesis two and three. It's the pride of the human race that began with our first parents' fall when they tried to figure God out *completely* and then came up with replacement gods that we *can* imagine! As a result of the description of the amazing God of the Bible, I believe that he clearly inspired that Book in order to reveal himself as the one only true mysterious God. He is the one who, I believe, rescued you from death in that horrible accident," I said as I picked up Joe's Bible.

"Bruce, my accident bruised and hair-line fractured my first vertebra. The doctors have given me their very pessimistic prognosis of permanent paralysis."

However, as Joe spoke about his prognosis, the pinky on his left hand began to move slightly—then his index finger and thumb. "Joe, you're moving! The 3-in-1 God is working in your body! He's definitely a God of surprises!"

He looked down at his hand with fixed, wide-open eyes and exclaimed, "Bruce, I believe that you're right!!"

CHAPTER 9

Mysterious Mathematics

Following our long pause in real reverie, Joe recovered his thinking to return to our conversation. He asked with the same kind of wonder, "But how can God be three persons, yet one God, as you say he is—if he does exist? In math 1+1+1=3. But you're saying that in God's math 1+1+1=1!"

"I'm afraid that the Mormons who have visited many Christian families are reported to have discovered that many professing Christians mistakenly believe that God is three Persons but *not* one God as the Mormons believe. However, the inspired Bible says clearly, but mysteriously, that he is *three* Persons revealed as only *one* God, an example of his *mysterious* mathematics. Joe, you've just experienced evidence of that 3-in-1 God's creative power giving you movement in your previously-paralyzed body!"

"I don't know, Bruce. The Bible's ideas are really hard to accept."

"Joe, in our Western culture *humanism* as a reliance on human beings and *rationalism* as a reliance on reason both rule supreme. As a result, western people rely on themselves and other people to try to figure everything out, even God. (Also, many Muslims say that Christian ideas do not pass the test of reason.)

"By contrast, on the basis of the Bible, I believe that God is beyond our reasoning ability as the mysterious, yet revealed, only true, 3-in-1 God. Why shouldn't he be? It was that same God who said in Isaiah 55:7,8 that he is a forgiving God and then continued, 'For my thoughts are not your thoughts, neither are your ways my ways...'. God is God, and I'm not. That fact is one of the many reasons that God has used to convince me that he inspired the Bible through ordinary people in order to reveal himself to us. That Book reveals the God who could never have been concocted by the human minds out of which came its writing. Why should we mere mortals think that we can understand our all-powerful Creator completely? That kind of pride was Adam and Eve's sin."

With his miraculous, newly-found ability to move and a big grin on his face, Stay-Puft-Marshmellow-Man Joe picked up a nearby Zoll Series-M Defibrillator paddle with his suddenly-moving, left-index finger and thumb. He turned it over with that same hand and spoke into it with a deep, dramatic tone as if he were a German-born, radio-talk-show host, "Here we have, l-ladies and g-gentlemen, the M-most R-right R-reverend Bruce Leiter, who declares that the one only true God is mysteriously revealed as three persons—the Father, Jesus, and Spirit—in one God, not three gods!"

"Yeah, you've got it, Joe!" I replied with my own big grin.

In response to his profound pronouncement, Joe lapsed into a long, silent pause as I pondered the unponderable. He broke the silence with a surprising decision, "I'll read the Book of John next."

CHAPTER 10

Good rehab torture

The next time I visited Joe, I had to search for him until I found him several blocks west in Davenport at the Genesis Medical Center, West Central Park, in the rehab wing, as he rested up from three full rehab hours.

"Hi, Bruce!" he said with a broad grin as I entered his room. "They torture me every day for three hours, but I have to admit that I'm getting back the use of my limbs. Besides physiatrists, other physical therapists, and social workers, they even have a spiritual-care person who dropped by. If God does exist, he seems to be pursuing me."

I didn't know how to respond to Joe's comment but asked, "How are you doing, Joe?"

"I'm tired physically and mentally, Bruce," he replied with a sigh.

"Yeah, it's a long haul," I intoned softly with an echoing sigh.

But unpredictable Joe brightened up with his announcement, "But I do have some good news, Bruce! They're going to let me go home from this prison as an ex-con by the end of the week, since I can now walk with a cane! Wanna see, Bruce?"

Before I had a chance to respond, he grabbed his four-pronged Invacare Medium-based Quad-Cane and hobbled from his bed near the window toward the hallway. "Ya know, the therapist even showed me the best way to use a cane. Ya hold the cane in the hand *opposite* your bad leg and move it forward as ya step with the bad foot to provide good balance. I always thought that ya move it on the *same side* as the bad leg *along with* the leg, the way the doctor in the TV show *House*—what's his name?—does it. It turns out that that's the *wrong way*. Isn't that a *hoot*?!"

"You seem to be in a good mood about going home, Joe."

"Yeah, I sure am!"

"Have you thought at all about our last conversation?" I asked as my voice lapsed into barely more than a whisper.

"Yeah, I don't see how God can be three Persons in one God. I'm still not convinced."

"That's OK, Joe," I rejoined. "We can *always* agree to disagree, can't we?"

"Yeah," Joe chimed in with a big grin. "What I can't understand is what John in his first chapter meant by the Word becoming flesh. How can God, a Spirit, become human?"

"Well, it's Christmas, Joe."

"No, it isn't, it's late June!"

I laughed at his face's funny gyrations. (One reason I really liked Joe was that his inner 'boy' connected with my inner 'boy.')

However, my reply tensed his muscles, "What I mean is, John 1:14 is John's description of Jesus' conception and birth that Christians celebrate at Christmas time. While remaining God—by the Holy Spirit from God the Father—the Word, the second Person of God, took on a perfect human nature through Mary without a human father."

"There's that three-in-one thing again," Joe said with a frown.

"No, three-Persons-in-one-*God*!" I corrected him with a grin.

"Well, I just can't buy it—not yet, anyway!" Joe exclaimed as he slapped his clenched right fist into his left hand.

"When, then? Anyway, you don't have to *buy it*, just *accept him*—if you want to."

Joe ignored my impishness, "But I must admit that those first four chapters in John's Gospel were pretty impressive. Jesus' declaration to a prim and proper Pharisee, Nicodemus, that God gave Jesus to us in order to give us a new birth; his healing of the cripple, who later turned Jesus in to the Pharisees; and his knowledge of the stranger, a Samaritan woman, are all amazing. However, I heard that the early church made up all of those stories and included them in the record. What do you say about that approach?" Joe asked with words like stinging sleet driven into the full length of my old body.

I repelled his stinging, friendly onslaught with another arrow-prayer, "Toward the end of the gospel in John 19:35, the Apostle John wrote about his eyewitness account of Jesus' death, 'The man who saw it has given testimony, and his testimony is true. He knows that he tells the truth, and he testifies so that you also may believe.' The truth of Jesus' life, death, and resurrection, the last of which shows that he is fully God with the Father, was John's true testimony. His persistent witness about those historic events, even while he faced the risk of his own suffering and death, caused his exile to the prison-island of Patmos.

"You and I would have given up and admitted that the story of Jesus' resurrection was false, if indeed we had made it up or had imagined it, under those circumstances. The fact that Jesus' followers persisted in testifying consistently to Jesus' life, death, and resurrection, even in the face of attacks on their very lives, is one reason that Jesus had to have risen from the grave and, therefore, has to be the God-man. I invite you to keep reading through to the Book of Acts, where you will see that the early church couldn't have made it all up. It's too amazing and mind-boggling to have been created by human minds!"

Joe slumped into his hospital recliner after his exhausting, limping journey a few times across the room and inquired with an accompanying frown, "If God showed people what to write in the Bible, why did he include all of that stuff in Genesis about the flood and Joseph's brothers' committing sexual sin and selling Joseph into slavery?"

"That's a good question, Joe. As you have read, God—those three persons in that one God—created everything good. But he is *not at all* to blame for human imperfections. It was the spread of sin that resulted in the flood and continued to be strong even in the lives of the ancestors of the Israelites, who were the human forebearers of David and Jesus. I believe that God inspired the Bible partly because no writers would have described, on their own, the ugly sins of their ancestors without God's direction.

"However, Jesus was the only flawless human. That same God is the Father, who created all things as well as you, Joe, through the second Person, Jesus, by the third Person, the Holy Spirit. However, the human race rebelled against their Creator. Doesn't it stand to reason that the God who created you has the right to claim and run your life, Joe, no matter how many objections you may have against his existence?"

Joe, who had been listening with his eyes fixed on me, fell silent for awhile. I guessed by Joe's silence that God, through my prayers and words, seemed to be making some progress with him. However, as the monster of unbelief raised its ugly head again, he said with his soap-opera-announcer's voice and with a sudden grin on his face, "First things first—*supper*!" as the gray-haired supper-woman entered his room.

I bowed out with the statement, "I'll leave you with your meal."

CHAPTER 11

Alarming news

Because I had agreed to bring Joe home that Friday, I arrived before noon at the rehab center. Joe gave me his cheery greeting, "Hi, Bruce. Ready to take me home? ...*Home*—what an inviting word!"

Just then, Joe clutched at the left side of his ample chest and gasped, "What's happening to me?!" as he slumped back into his hospital bed.

Greatly alarmed, I asked, "What's wrong, Joe?!"

He groaned in return, "I've got a lot of chest pain!"

I called the nurse. The hospital personnel called a doctor, who examined him with the observation, "Well, he doesn't have the usual symptoms of a heart attack, but I'm sending him to the Genesis, East Rusholme, Chest Pain Observation Unit, just to be sure."

I volunteered to take him there. However, he writhed in agony with every bump on that pest-of-a-street that we had to travel toward Genesis, East Rusholme Street. Those three rectangular "monster-eyes" on that building seemed strangely inviting this time. The staff then rushed Joe into an observation room, where they did all of the tests for a heart attack.

After what seemed like an eternity of waiting, the doctor in charge, a kindly, middle-aged, graying man, entered Joe's room and stated in a matter-of-fact tone, "We find no evidence of a heart attack. Mr. Smith, I suggest that you seek a psychological solution."

Joe exclaimed with his eyes wide-open and his body arching away from the doctor, "You mean, you want me to see a *shrink*!?"

"All I know is that there is no physical cause for your chest pain. I've seen many other people with severe chest pain that have had many losses and traumas in their lives. Those people are actually experiencing anxiety attacks that look a lot like heart attacks with pain similar to yours."

"Well, I'm not going to a shrink. I'm not crazy! I'll just be less anxious, instead."

The doctor replied with a note of warning in his voice, "Suit yourself, but you'll probably have more anxiety attacks unless you find out and deal with the underlying psychological foundation."

CHAPTER 12

A very helpful group

As Joe and I drove the by-now-all-too-familiar trip home, I gently described the severe chest pain that I had experienced twice when we lived in Oak Harbor, Washington, "Joe, I had two severe attacks that mimicked heart attacks."

Joe stated with a wave of his left hand, "Fire away, Bruce. We have time."

"In the middle of the night, I awoke with horrible, stabbing chest pain. While Winnie called 9-1-1, I got dressed. Every movement shot severe pain throughout my upper chest. Then, as I rode twelve miles in the ambulance on Whidbey Island to Coupeville Hospital, every bump in the road sent more excruciating pain throughout my chest. After I spent a long, sleepless night of observation in Intensive Care, the doctor in charge the next morning said about the same thing that the Genesis doctor said.

"I then found a psychiatrist who just listened to me but didn't help me for six whole months. Frustrated, I then went to another psychiatrist, who developed a plan of action for me but wrongly diagnosed me as manic-depressive, the same diagnosis that they call 'bipolar' these days. (It turned out later that I had been suffering from the disease of depression for seven years.)

"Anyway, I ended up as a patient at Pine Rest Christian Mental Health in Grand Rapids, Michigan, for four weeks, during which God's healing of my depression began in April and May of 1986. I'm sorry, Joe. I'm going on and on."

"Not at all, Bruce. Please tell me about your experiences at the mental hospital. You weren't crazy, were you?"

I laughed, "No, Joe. Depression isn't craziness with uncontrolled actions—just the reverse. About 80% of depressed people have bottled up their anger inside of them. However, my symptom of that mental disease was physical tiredness that escalated into exhaustion and finally resulted in an emotional shut-down.

"It all began when I got tired climbing the steps to the third floor at the Calvin College library during my senior year at Calvin Seminary. The first doctor said that if I just started exercising—walking, biking, or running—I would be fine. Well, exercise, while good for me, didn't help my tiredness. During my first six years in the ministry, I became more and more exhausted. Finally, I ended up retiring from ministry and flying to the mental hospital in Michigan, which was the place of God's first breakthrough in group therapy...."

"Bruce, what's group therapy?"

"It's a situation where two therapists sit in a circle with about five or six patients who have similar struggles. They ask each patient how they feel that day. When it was my turn to describe my feelings, tears began to form in my eyes as I struggled to say, 'I feel..., I feel....' To free me up, one of the therapists asked a particularly-empathetic female patient, a heavy-set brunette, to sit behind me facing the same way with her hands on my shoulders. The therapist inquired of the other patient what my feelings were, since my anger and anxiety were bottled up inside me.

"Suddenly the 'bottle' burst as my tears flowed non-stop down my cheeks. Those relieving tears flowed freely even though my mom had taught me that 'big boys don't cry,' a very unhealthy teaching during my forty-three years to that point. At the same time the other patient was voicing *my* feelings, 'I'm lonely so *far* from my family....I'm angry at other people for things they've done...and at God for my son's death!'

"The group offered me a tissue, but I refused it because I sensed, somehow, that it would stop the cleansing flow of pent-up emotions. I sensed that the group-therapy session was the 3-in-1 God's breakthrough to begin his healing of my anxious and angry emotions.

"Anyway, the bell ending our session rang, but I unashamedly continued to let the flood of tears flow unchecked down my face. Then, I took over for the other patient, 'Yeah, I'm angry at my God! Why did he allow us to go through almost three years of Keith's sickness, get hepatitus, experience his death, and let me grieve fourteen years, the last seven in deepening depression? Why, God?! My prayers just seem to bounce off the ceiling!'"

I continued my description of my Pine Rest experience, "Our therapy group also spent time in what is called 'psychodrama.'" Joe turned and looked at me with raised eyebrows as I continued, "That session was a time when patients voluntarily practiced their anger in appropriate ways for the time after their discharge. Because I was a non-assertive person up until that stage of my life, I didn't *want* to do it. However, I knew that I *had* to do psychodrama. I slowly raised my hand to volunteer during one session in my fourth week at Pine Rest. Other patients volunteered to play the people that I had to confront about their unloving actions. After a little while the instructor said, 'You're getting too cerebral. Clear the stage, everyone. Now, just stand there, Bruce.'"

CHAPTER 13

Amazing drama

"What happened then?"

"Tears were gathering in my eyes and on my cheeks when the instructor said, 'You're mad at God, aren't you?'"

"Immediately, I agreed with hoarse intensity, 'Yeah, I'm mad at God!'

"Where is God right now, Bruce?"

"I responded with equal intensity but with a smile, 'He's right here beside me!'

"He inquired with a note of surprise in his voice, 'What's he doing now?'

"I exclaimed immediately, 'He's hugging me!'

"Recovering from his surprise, the instructor asked for patient-volunteers to represent God to me. Interestingly, three patients volunteered to go up on the one-step-high stage, hug me, and say, 'I love you....I love you....I love you.' I know that it was the Father, Jesus, and Holy Spirit, the one-only-true God in three Persons, fervently hugging me through those patients! Stunned, the middle-aged instructor concluded the session by saying, 'In all my years leading these sessions, I've never experienced anything like *that* drama!' I sensed that it was my Triune God who had accepted me and come close to me when people would have fled my anger."

"That's amazing, Bruce!" said Joe, raising his face and lifting his hands with palms up. "Did anything else happen to you at Pine Rest?"

"Well, the staff referred me to the Biofeedback guy. He had a stress-measuring machine that showed that I was stressed out with my depression-anger. He taught me to breathe *in* very slowly, with my abdomen going *out*. When I exhaled, I was to breathe *out* very slowly with my abs going *in* as I let the tension in my muscles go. When I breathed out, I shouldn't even hear myself breathing. He recommended that I think the word 'calm' as I breathed out and released the stress.

"Well, I thought that just thinking one word was boring. As a result (I'm sure with God's leading), I instead prayed breathing-prayers *very slowly* to lower my stress level; to fall asleep at night; and, at the same time, to talk to the only true, 3-in-1 God with two-syllable words and phrases like '**Fa**[abdomen going *out*, while breathing *in*]-**ther**[abdomen going *in*, while slowly breathing *out*], **Je**[abdomen *out*, breathing *in*]-**sus** [abdomen *in*, breathing *out*], **Spir**[abs *out*]-**it**[abs *in*], **one**[*out*] **God**[*in*], **calm**[*out*] **me**[*in*], **make**[*out*] **me**[*in*] **so**[*out*] **calm**[*in*], and with other pairs of words and syllables."

Joe inquired, "Do you still do those prayers to relax, Bruce?" In response to my nodding head, Joe continued, "I wonder if *I'm* depressed as you were, because I *have* been feeling very tired lately."

"Well, you've certainly have had more than enough to be depressed about!"

* * *

"Then Jesus came to them and said, 'All authority in heaven and on earth has been given to me. Therefore go and make disciples of all nations, baptizing them in the name of the Father and of the Son and of the Holy Spirit, and teaching them to obey everything I have commanded you. And surely I am with you always, to the very end of the age.'"

(Matthew 28:18-20).

Part Two Questions

1. During the discussion following the Cub game, how did the narrator and Joe remain friends, while disagreeing about God and the Bible? What challenge did Joe accept? How can we discuss Christian beliefs with Christians and non-Christians alike without building walls between us? What qualities do we need in order to discuss beliefs without driving a wedge between us and unbelievers? How can we develop those qualities?

2. How effective was the narrator's testimony about his son's faith? How can we share personal testimonies about our experiences with God and be sure to give him the credit?

3. What is your opinion of the narrator's idea that he shared after Joe's statement that he didn't think that there's "anything beyond death"? How convincing is the narrator's assertion that God had to have revealed himself in the Bible because he is beyond human thought? What reasons can you develop to support the fact that God revealed himself in the Bible and in creation?

4. How convincing do you find the narrator's answers to Joe's ideas about the creation account in Genesis? What other observations could he have made?

5. What testimony of the narrator changes Joe's reactions from skeptical questioning to enthusiasm? What testimonies do you have to God's work in changing your life? Which idea of the narrator results in Joe's silence? Why do you suppose that he is silent?

6. What traumatic phone call ends chapter 2? How has God used traumatic events in your life or in others' lives that you know to bring good out of those events?

PART 3

Who Is the True God?

CHAPTER 14

Imperfections

As I approached the exercise facility after leaving my car on one particularly-hot, humid August Monday afternoon that was good for growing Iowa corn, I spied Joe limping with his cane to the door from the opposite direction. He had gamely walked the few short, small-town blocks from his parents' home instead of driving. He greeted me like some long-lost relative, "Hi, buddy! How's it goin'?"

"It's goin' great, fellow traveler! You were walkin' today?!"

He put his hand up to his mouth and whispered loudly, "Yeah, I gotta get with it, don't ya know!"

"What on earth are ya sayin'?"

He looked like a happy puppy. "Ya know, goin' green!" He opened the right side of the double-doors for me, while flourishing his non-existent, feathery Musketeer's hat and balancing his wide body precariously on his cane.

We entered the men's beige locker room as I mustered a question, "You appear to be doing well. Are you in as good a mood as you appear to be?"

Joe lapsed into his favorite English dialect, "I feel just tip-top, my dear chap!"

My response was a little hesitant and non-committal, "Well,...I hope that you're doing...OK. It's a great day to be alive, as they all are."

"That's for sure!" However, his next question, after he paused for dramatic effect, just about floored me, "Bruce, why do you believe in sin?"

I recovered with God's help and answered my suddenly-serious friend, "Uh, I don't 'believe' in sin as in 'trust' in it. I believe that sin is very real in all of us and that it exists because of Genesis chapter three and Psalm 51 as well as many other Bible passages. Adam and Eve started sin for humans after, of course, Satan started it for many of the angels who followed him in his rebellion against God."

Joe's objection launched like a missile sent to create a torpedo, terrorist explosion aimed at the Bible, "But aren't all those so-called 'sins' merely mistakes or errors-in-judgment caused by society or our parents, for which we have no responsibility?"

"No, Joe, I don't believe so. Though factors like family or other influences may help us understand people's sins, I believe, on the basis of the Bible, that not one of people's actions, no matter how understandable, justifies our sins. I believe in understanding and loving sinners, while not excusing sin, starting with me. The Bible says in Ezekiel 18:20, 'The one who sins is the one who will die,' not our parents or the world around us. We need to be punished for our own sins, since God is the perfectly-just Judge."

Joe's attacking barrage continued, "Well then, why doesn't God—if he does exist—immediately punish sin, if there is such a thing? Why does he let crooked politicians, terrorists, and mass murderers get away with murder figuratively and literally?"

I leaned forward on the bench near Joe's locker, "The writer of Psalm 73 had a similar question and almost lost his faith in God because of it until he entered God's house, the church of his day. There, he learned that all public and hidden sinners—that's all of us—leave everything and everyone behind when they die. Then they will face God's judgment.

"Joe, can you imagine a perfect God letting us dirty, imperfect people into his perfect place called heaven? That kind of unlikely action would be like a neat, cleanly mother letting her muddy young son traipse around her just-cleaned house, getting everything dirty and messy after he entered the house from a muddy stream where he had been playing. That just wouldn't happen. Instead, she would send him to the tub to get clean.

"God-man Jesus' perfect life and death clean up believers just like cleansing water. The result is that God the Father accepts them in his perfect presence."

As we headed toward the shower-room, Joe opened his eyes wide and exclaimed, "Yeah, I'm sure that our moms would've sent us to get cleaned up before we dirtied their precious homes!"

"Speak only for your mom! Mine was probably the worst housekeeper ever!" I opined with thumbs turned down.

"O, Bruce, you don't really mean what you just said about your mother, do you?" Joe asked with furrowed brows.

"I certainly do! She had a kind, generous heart as a believer, but she didn't do her housekeeping! However, my point is that God doesn't have the imperfections of our parents. (Moms are often cleanly because of perfectionist pride, also a sin.) He's a just God in rightly punishing human imperfection since he's completely perfect and rightly expects it of us, his creatures.

"According to the Bible, our sins are defined as the self-centeredness in all of us when we were conceived and born that sometimes comes out in our self-centered actions."

Joe's round face crinkled up, as the full force of the pre-swim stream hit his full face, "You mean, sin isn't just actions?!"

"You probably think that sin only happens in the big city, rarely in small towns, and only in outward actions? No, Joe. Sin as human selfishness also happens in small towns, rural areas, and here," as I pointed with my long, wide, right-index finger toward my heart. "The Bible also says in Jeremiah 17:9, 'The heart is deceitful above all things and beyond cure. Who can understand it?' Jeremiah goes on to quote God, who says, 'I the LORD search the heart and examine the mind, to reward everyone according to their conduct....' Only the perfect conduct and death of Jesus as believers' substitute earn God the Father's approval for those who trust in him."

Joe reacted with crossed arms, "I get what you believe. But what I don't understand is this: How can small-town and rural folks be sinners, Bruce?"

"Well, in my experience with the wonderful people in those places, there exists a lot of people-pleasing. I understand the people-pleasing approach because I'm a recovering people-pleaser. That quality is almost always a selfish desire for overcoming our insecurity in order to feel good about ourselves, while we attempt to protect our reputations at all costs. The result is that we do actions that will make other people like us. That self-centered desire to please people is just as much sin as the more-obvious ready-rebellion of some big-city people.

"The reason is that it's just one part of the religion of humanism, which depends on other people for satisfaction in life. The Bible shows that people are conceived and born as either ready-rebels or people-pleasers. Both types are sinners leading self-centered lives until God reveals himself to them.

"For example, Joe, human sin is something like cats and dogs...."

Joe stopped me with one his "Joeisms," "Say *what!?*"

I grinned with my inner impishness showing through, "*What!*"

Then Joe caught on to my joke and asked in his most-pompous tone, "What do ye mean, Right Reverend Sir?"

I gave him our family's example, "We had a pet cat once which moved with us to the West Coast between my first two churches. During the two years when we lived in the Puget Sound on Whidbey Island, a woman who trained little orange Pomeranians gave us an 'imperfect' Pom-Pom pup. Our son Mike named him Prang after a pretend dog on an imaginary planet, since he was into science fiction at the time.

"Anyway, the cat, which thought that it owned our house as its territory, was bigger than that pup and, thus, tried to dominate him. However, that little dog stood up for his rights as part of the family. They would sail across the living room floor in the sprawling, ranch-style parsonage from opposite directions, stand on their back paws, punch at each other as if they were boxers, and then sail off in the directions from which they had first come. They were part of our family entertainment! The cat eventually became queen of the heights, and the dog was king of the floor.

"It was my observation that cats tend to be more like ready-rebel humans, while dogs seem to be more like people-pleasers. Similarly, both human approaches are self-centered ways to deal with life. Both need repentance, that is, a change in our whole personalities, which only the 3-in-1 God can cause permanently in believers."

Joe's gaze had been riveted on me. When I finished talking, his face lit up suddenly as if a light had just gone on in his brain as we approached the cleansing, chlorinated pool through the swinging door from the locker room, "So sin is a matter of selfish inner desires *and* outer actions, as we spend our whole lives like either cats or dogs?!" Responding to my nodding head, Joe continued, "Well, then, all of us are sinners. Why doesn't God send us all to hell—if there is such a place—as my Sunday and Bible school teachers said?"

Just before I eased into the pool inch by inch feet-first, I emphasized, "My friend, we escape only because of his gift of the God-man Jesus' death on the cross as the free path to God's acceptance through faith in him!"

A half an hour later, Joe and I were lounging stretched out in the relaxing spa when my friend Joe suddenly shot another friendly but menacing missile at me, "Bruce, how could God hold Adam's and Eve's eating of the fruit against them when the devil made them do it—if that story really happened?"

CHAPTER 15

More imperfections

My quiet response in our soothing hot-place made my friend sit up straight, "A lot of people have tried to blame the devil or someone else for their own thoughts, decisions, and actions just as Adam and Eve did, as you will remember from Genesis chapter three. For example, when God sought and confronted Adam about disobeying his command not to eat the forbidden fruit, he played the blame game by saying in Genesis 3:12, 'The *woman you* put here with me—she gave me some fruit from the tree, and I ate it.' Did you notice that Adam blamed Eve *and* God for his selfish disobedience rather than himself?"

We then noticed for the first time a swimmer doing the breaststroke in the pool. Joe suddenly opened his eyes and mouth wide, "I wonder who that woman is."

Then, we returned to our conversation with my comment, "Joe, other influences that have led us to self-centered sin are no excuses. The fact is that Adam and Eve could have chosen to reject those temptations. Similarly, we also have full responsibility for all of our thoughts, desires, emotions, words, and actions. We will all answer to God, the Judge, for all of them, because he knows every one of them."

Shocked Joe turned his thumbs upward and exclaimed, "Ya mean that God's not preparin' gifts for me as my great Santa in the sky 'cause of how good I've been?!"

I answered, "Definitely not!" Joe's mouth went to the north as his eyes and forehead went south. I shook my head at the funny fellow in the hot-tub's opposite corner.

Our two-way conversation suddenly changed when the other swimmer—a blond-haired, blue-eyed, shapely young woman wearing a light-blue, one-piece swimsuit—entered the hot-tub after her swim. I moved to the southeast corner to make room for her and offered my hand with the comment, "I don't believe we've met. I'm Bruce Leiter. You are...?"

CHAPTER 16

A hot-tub arrival

The thirty-something woman put her dainty, young hand into my large, aging hand and shook it with a firm grip as she observed, "I'm Holly Holmes." Turning to Joe, she asked, "You look vaguely familiar. Your name is...?"

Joe blushed many shades of red as he barely managed, "I'm Joe Smith," and shook her hand.

Holly abruptly introduced herself before either of us could ask her any questions, "Now, before you guys start commenting on my name, first, I want to let you know that, yes, I was born on Christmas Day—a real bummer! That timing resulted in my first name. Second, my parents met for the first time at a poetry reading at college. That meeting is the reason that my name is alliterative. Third, I am definitely *not* descended from Sherlock. He was fictional, but I'm not!"

Joe's eyes glazed over while he stared at her, "You sure *aren't* fictional!"

Holly continued with her high-pitched voice while ignoring Joe's stare, "Have you guys been coming to the pool a long time?"

"I guess it's been about a month or two, hasn't it, Joe?"

Joe croaked with a squeak and a smile, "Yeah, I guess so. Time moves really fast when you're havin' fun!"

"Yeah, that's right, Joe! What brings you to our small town and to the pool, Holly?"

Holly answered immediately with a big, beautiful smile, "I grew up here, went off to Chicago to work, discovered that I didn't care for the city *rat-race*, and got a job on this side of the Quad-Cities so that I could return to my 'roots' here."

Joe commented, "Yeah, I hate those big-city *runs* too!"

* * *

Two weeks later Holly, Joe, and I converged at the exercise place on a sunny, blue-sky day. As I parked and lifted myself with effort out of my car, I suddenly spied Joe and Holly gesturing dramatically in serious conversation on the sidewalk leading to the front door. As I approached them, I shouted a friendly greeting, "Hey, how's it going?"

Joe saluted with his right hand, "It's going fine, Bruce."

Holly echoed Joe with her smile, "Yeah, fine."

We entered the front door together as Joe held it for both of us with a flourish and a comic bow, "After you, lady and gentleman!"

Holly laughed loudly and I chuckled quietly, while we parted as men to the left and a woman to the right to put on our swimming suits in our respective locker rooms.

I paused in front of Joe's locker to ask the inevitable question, "So, what were you and Holly talking about out there?"

Joe paused to make the most of the moment in his usual comical way, "We were talkin'…about the *weather*!" In response to my seriousness, he immediately corrected his statement, "If you must know, I asked her for a date on Saturday night. We're going to a movie at the only theater in this one-horse town."

I replied with a wink, "I hope you have a nice time."

As we meandered, staring at the rafters, from in the locker room and shower to the pool, we looked down to see that Holly was already doing her watery, wearying laps. When Joe and I finished swimming, our three-way, hot-tub chatter began with my friendly question for Holly, "So, besides swimming, what do you like to do to have fun, Holly?"

"I enjoy watching both baseball and basketball and playing golf."

Joe exclaimed, "You're a sports fan?!"

"Yeah, I've been an Iowa Hawkeye fan all my life, started watching the Chicago Bulls when Michael Jordan was playing, and suffer with the Chicago Cubs. I was always something of a tomboy playing baseball and basketball with the boys. When our family got cable TV during my childhood, I used to share the Cub games with my father during the summer. Previously, we could only get them on our radio. The rest of our family wasn't interested. It was a father-daughter time."

I replied, "We're going to get along just fine! Joe and I are Cub fans too!"

Joe jumped in quickly, "Holly, Bruce and I disagree agreeably on religion. What is your church background?"

She explained, "I was raised a Catholic but became disillusioned with the church because I discovered that priests molested boys and that the church covered that sin up."

"I understand, Holly," I empathized. "When I was a boy, one of our pastors invited young boys to go the drive-in theater with him and molested them there. He even tried to touch my older brother in the wrong places while they were sitting in our living room when my mother was in the kitchen. When the pastor tried to touch my brother, he punched him hard. Mom came into the room and asked what happened to the pastor, who was out cold on the floor. When my brother told her, she kicked him out of the house when he awoke and started a campaign in the church to get rid of him. Sadly, he accepted a call to another church. If that sin had happened today, the church would have called the police, kicked him out of the ministry, and made him get counseling."

Holly stated, "Yeah, I'm skeptical of the church's authority and teachings now."

Joe replied, "I can understand your feelings, Holly."

CHAPTER 17

A *"Routine"* Morning Errand

About 11:00 A.M. on a routine Saturday morning, I visited a local bank to do the usual high-finance transactions made by retired people with pensions and Social Security. Our bank, Community Trust, was at the north end of the business district on Main Street. East of the bank was a gray three-story apartment house beyond the drive-through. A white, older, two-story home beyond the parking spaces was on the north side.

I entered the front door; acknowledged Holly, who had arrived a few minutes earlier and was standing at the desk provided for our writing benefit, and teetered there on my two painful feet. My friend Joe entered with his usual fractured flourish and greeted both of us with his surprised, jolly, small-town friendliness, "Hi, Holly and Bruce! Whazzup?"

Our neighborly reply was interrupted when three men in ski-masks rushed into the bank and shut all of the tan vertical blinds on the front, wall-length windows. The tallest man shot into the ceiling with his assault rifle. The shortest man of the three culprits shouted with his high-pitched voice at the top of his lungs, "No one move! Hands up! You won't get hurt if you do everything we say. Now, everyone, get on the floor with your hands where we can see them."

Joe froze in place, while Holly and I sprawled on the carpet. The short man waved his gun and screamed at him, "Are you hard of hearing, or what?!"

Joe turned slowly toward him and asked calmly with his best puppy-dog look, "I'm confused. You said for me not to move, put my hands in the air, *and* get on the floor. Which one of those three actions do you *really* want me to do?"

The short bank robber shoved Joe so violently that he lost his balance and landed on my middle, which was already prone with the rest of me. The robber delivered his sarcastic speech, "Hey, we've got a comedian here! You folks don't have to be scared. We just came to get our share of the stimulus funds from a bank that the feds helped!"

He turned away from the four customers and two employees stretched out aimlessly on the brown, carpeted floor and headed toward the manager's office, as the third bank robber kept watch over us.

Before the shortest man could escort the female manager, who rose from her humiliating position on the floor, to the vault, a loud, amplified voice pierced the tense atmosphere of the bank, "Attention, all of you in the bank, this is the police chief speaking. We have you surrounded. Surrender and none of you will be hurt. Send the hostages out first."

The tallest man exclaimed with a high-pitched shriek, "Hey, Mac, we're going to get caught and go away for a long time! What are we going to do?!" and ran with fluid motions like an athlete several yards to the shortest man, who turned away from the front entrance and assured him, "Remember, we talked about this possibility. We still have Plan B." Armed with a shotgun, the shortest man turned to shove the manager, a middle-aged, graying woman with a slight build, toward the vault with the urgent command, "Get us the money!"

Meanwhile, Joe whispered secretly to me, "I have a bad feeling in my bones about this robbery, given everything else that has happened to me recently!"

I shot a whisper back at him with a slight grin, "Personally, I'm praying with my *mind*, but I feel something else in my *bones* that doesn't have a lot to do with the robbery!"

Joe also managed a partial grin as he whispered, "Yeah, I guess that my body is a little like a big sack of potatoes."

"Well, it's certainly not like a big bag of potato *chips*!"

Holly, who had fallen a few feet away, whispered, "Yeah, Joe, you're feather-light!"

The tallest robber noticed our deep conversation, stopped it by jabbing all of us with his gun, and yelled at us, "Stop your whispering!"

CHAPTER 18

Help from above

The next series of events happened in rapid succession. The three serious, stimulus "Stooges" let the manager, an employee, and a customer go out the front door as a diversion. Then, they put a large amount of "stimulus" cash in their briefcase. Their Plan B involved putting their three guns to the heads of Holly, Joe, and me; exiting with us ahead of them out of the back door like three cows being prodded toward slaughter in a meat-packing plant; and leading us past the north side of Peaceful Valley Apartments for their escape to their van on the next street to the east.

Suddenly, as the escape was underway and as we passed the north side of the apartment house, a whirring sound came from the sky just above the apartment-house's roof and gutter. A helicopter swooped down from the beautiful, blue Iowa sky. Three rapid sniper shots with three "righteous kills" ended forever the would-be Stooge-robbers' attempt at being stimulated.

Holly, Joe, and I hugged each other for a couple of minutes until our trembling stopped, while hundred-dollar bills rained down on us. Shortly, two police officers approached us to make sure that we were all right. We pinched each other's arms and legs to make sure that we were alive and intact.

Holly said to Joe and me when she had regained some composure, "I'm sure glad that these great people rescued us!"

My response was, "I'm thankful that God answered my prayers, Holly."

Joe replied, "I'm just happy that we're all safe!" An ambulance whisked us to the local hospital for a precautionary checkup inspite of our protests. During that brief trip, I called Winnie to inform her about our hair-raising "adventure." In response, her voice sounded both scared and relieved at the same time, "I thank God that everyone's OK!"

Early on that afternoon our condo phone almost broke its cradle with many requests from the media as far away as Chicago and Omaha. News of the aborted bank theft had traveled as quickly as news on the Internet. I scheduled the interviews with the reporters who were within driving distance for later Saturday afternoon and evening. We invited Joe and Holly to our house to talk to the media.

Our first visitor at mid-afternoon was Deputy Sheriff Dave Wilkins, a thirty-something fellow with close-cropped hair, who asked us how we were doing and shared his part in our escapade, "The military trained me as a sharpshooter. As a result, part of our plan was to use the helicopter that the hospital just got, courtesy of the stimulus funds from the federal government through our Iowa governor." Joe, Holly, and I winked at each other as he continued, "We decided to use the chopper to prevent the success of any hostage-taking or robbery in our county. Therefore, when the alarm from the bank came in, the pilot and I swung into action. The rest is history."

All three of us rose in unison to thank Dave with hearty handshakes. Joe summed up our feelings, "Thank you so much for your rescue. I was scared that if we had reached that van, we were toast!"

He responded with firm handshakes, "You're very welcome!"

That afternoon and evening the three of us endured reporters' questions as our condo parking lot looked like an RV park at the height of the summer season with satellite dishes sprouted all over it.

The story all over the nightly news was about peace-shattering events in a sleepy, quiet Iowa town that ended with a sudden, dramatic intervention by the local police. News reporters had also discovered that the hostage-taking thieves were out-of-work guys from East Moline, Illinois, one of the five "Quad-Cities" that all straddle the Mississippi River on the Illinois and Iowa sides. They had worked in the John Deere factory in Moline, Illinois.

CHAPTER 19

Debriefing

Because of the glut of media interviews that Holly, Joe, and I endured at the condo Saturday, we decided to escape, as usual, to unwind in the solitude of the pool Monday afternoon. Holly was already in the hot-tub when we settled into that peaceful place after an invigorating, stress-relieving series of laps. We greeted her like some long-lost relative. She asked, "Joe and Bruce, how are you fellas doing?"

Joe admitted, "I was scared Saturday!"

I replied, "I sure was too! I'm doing about as well as can be expected, Holly. I'm thankful that no one in the bank was hurt or killed. God was definitely with us. How are you doing, Holly?"

Holly responded, "I'm still a little shaken. I shudder to think what might've happened to us if the thieves had escaped with us in their van!"

Joe agreed, "Yeah, it's really scary to imagine." At that point Joe came up with a surprising question, "We were talking about sin what seems like an eternity ago. Weren't those three ne'er-do-wells the sinners, while we were the innocent victims?"

I mentally sent up a prayer, "What do you think, Holly?"

She pursed her lips, "We're all far from perfect, Joe."

I chimed in, "Joe, from a human point-of-view you're right. However, from God's viewpoint we are just as much sinners as they were, because we all tend to be selfish. Those robbers and we will all give account to God about our whole lives when we die as well as during the Final Judgment. I believe that the only basis on which God will judge all sinful humans will be whether or not we trusted only in Jesus as our personal Rescuer and the Road to God the Father. It's only because of our trust in Jesus' rescue that we have any hope that we will last forever with him. It seems to me that God used earthly rescuers to rescue our lives yesterday. However, Jesus is our only true Rescuer for this life *and* the next."

Holly said, "I used to have those beliefs in the Catholic church, but when it came to light that priests were molesting boys and the church covered it up, I stopped going. I'm not sure anymore about those priests' teachings."

I leaned forward, "I can understand your anger, Holly. People do disappoint us."

Joe also leaned forward, "The claim that we're all sinners is so different from usual human thinking! It just seems to me that those crooks were the sinners, not us." Then, my comic friend surfaced, "You're sure that you didn't make up that strange idea?"

I retorted with a half-grin, "No, Joe, I found it in the Bible! The fact that that Book presents such ideas that are so strange to the human ear shows me that it had to be inspired by God. Therefore, its teaching about all humans' sinfulness has to be true."

Holly observed, "That idea is interesting, Bruce."

Joe screwed up his face and uttered a "Joeism" that was a little like a TV comedian from the past Gary Coleman, "Whatcha talkin' about, preacher-man?!"

* * *

At one time we too were foolish, disobedient, deceived and enslaved by all kinds of passions and pleasures. We lived in malice and envy, being hated and hating one another. But when the kindness and love of God our Savior appeared, he saved us, not because of righteous things we had done, but because of his mercy. He saved us through the washing of rebirth and renewal by the Holy Spirit, whom he poured out on us generously through Jesus Christ our Savior, so that, having been justified by his grace, we might become heirs having the hope of eternal life.

(Titus 3:3-7)

Part Three Questions

1. What do the prayers, impatience, and questions of the narrator during his trip to visit Joe show about him?

2. What description of Joe reveals the origin of the title of this book? How appropriate do you think that the reference to the movie is? What comparisons could be made between doubts and ghosts? Why is any comparison helpful to you? Or isn't it? Why not?

3. Why is the narrator suddenly without answers when Joe asks why the accident happened? What interpretation did he then give about that event? What is the difference between saying that "you should believe" and "I'm sure glad that God…?" Which kind of statement to an unbeliever is more appropriate? Why?

4. Why is the narrator's question about reading the Bible and/or praying for Joe appropriate? Or don't you think so? Why?

5. What is your reaction to the narrator's explanation of the 3-in-1 God? How effective is that explanation? How does that explanation affect your faith in that same God?

PART 4

Why are the Bible and Jesus important?

CHAPTER 20

An Important Book

The next time Holly, Joe, and I saw each other was at the swimming pool in late September. Holly and I were doing our laps when Joe shuffled slowly from the locker room with a grin a little like Tim Conway's old man on the *Carol Burnett Show*, minus the stringy white hair. I waved at him with a wide grin as I made my turn. Holly and I waited for him to enter the hot-tub and greeted him, "How're ya doing, Joe?"

He responded, as he slowly slid his ample body into the welcoming warmth, "OK, Bruce. Hi, Holly."

Holly asked, "Hi, Joe. So..., how's your physical therapy coming along?"

He slumped into his familiar spot in the northeast corner of the spa, "I don't see many signs of progress, but my therapist does."

"How...are ya doing...emotionally?" I ventured while lowering my voice.

He imitated my lowered voice with uncharacteristic irritation, "Well, I haven't gotten a shrink, if that's what you're asking. I'm doing OK, considering all that I've—we've—gone through lately."

We sat silently for several seconds that seemed like a long time, until we let him break the silence as a grin crossed his chubby face, "How about those Cubbies? I think you're right that this is finally the year!"

After other small talk Joe's skepticism said, "Bruce, I've been reading the Gospel of John. What's up with Jesus' claims that he's God? No human being can make that claim unless he's crazy!"

Holly chimed in, "Yeah, Bruce, I wonder the same thing. The Catholic teaching that Mary was sinless also seems unrealistic."

I answered, "As far as I'm concerned, his claims that he's God are found in his statements, 'I AM...the bread of life, ...the light of the world, ...the good shepherd, and...the resurrection and the life.' He also claimed, 'Before Abraham was, I am.' Those claims identified him with the 3-in-1 LORD who revealed himself in Exodus chapter three to Moses in the burning bush that didn't burn up. There, God said that his name is 'I AM THAT I AM.' With such claims, Jesus was either mentally-ill or truly God. I don't see how some people can claim that he's only a good teacher or prophet and nothing more."

Joe agreed, "Yeah, how can they make that claim, given what Jesus says about himself?" Holly nodded her head.

"Hey, all of us agree about something in spiritual matters!"

Holly and Joe said simultaneously, "Yeah!"

Holly's and Joe's eyes opened wide in response to my next comment, "However, it seems to me that Jesus backed up his claims by feeding more than 5,000 people with a few loaves and fish in chapter six, healing the man born blind in chapter nine, and raising Lazarus from the dead in chapter eleven! Those miracles alone show me that he's the Creator of our food, eyes, and lives, along with the Father and the Holy Spirit! Jesus performed *major* miracles for the crowds that followed him, on the man born without even eye-equipment, and for the man who was dead for four days!

"Furthermore, God used Jesus' death to lift from believers the curse on all of us that God justly pronounced on all humans, as you've read, Joe, in Genesis chapter three. Moreover, Jesus' resurrection, witnessed by over 500 believers at one time and by smaller groups on several other occasions over a 40-day period, gave all believers new life. I'm convinced that none of those events could've come from human thinking and therefore they demonstrate definitely, in my mind, that he *had* to be God in the flesh. As a result, God definitely *inspired* the Bible because no one could have dreamed up Jesus' claims and miracles! Furthermore, I don't find Mary's sinlessness in the Bible."

Joe was so wrapped up in my words swirling into his ears that he slowly sank so far into the bubbling hot water like a turtle sinking into quicksand that Holly had to remind him with a quiet voice, "Joe, you're sinking."

CHAPTER 20

A great book about a free gift

With a grin, Joe grabbed the side of the tub, pulled himself up, and responded, "However, I just can't see how those words could have been from God."

"Joe, there are several other reasons I can see that the Bible is inspired. The fact that the Bible is as realistic as it is about the sins of the 'heroes of faith' shows me that it had to have come from God. For example, King David, described as being 'a man after God's own heart,' nevertheless committed adultery with Bathsheba and engineered her husband's murder in warfare, thus breaking several of the Ten Commandments. Holly, people like David and even the church will disappoint us with their many imperfections, but God is faithful.

"Other national histories of that day always thoroughly 'whitewashed' their national heroes because they claimed to be gods. However, the Bible said it the way it was very honestly, to show that the God who inspired that Book is the God of grace."

Joe responded, "Run that idea by me again."

I rose to the edge of the hot-tub, "God's grace is God's free, undeserved acceptance of believers. For me, grace is another evidence of the Bible's inspiration, because it is almost always alien to humans' treatment of each other. People's usual selfish actions happen even sometimes, sadly, in the church!

"My point, Joe and Holly, is that the Bible says that we can't earn his love by being good! He gives his undeserved love freely. Grace, a quality that is completely foreign to human performance-oriented thought, is God's acceptance of believers earned only by Jesus' perfect life, not ours, and his death on the cross. All of the other spiritual groups, including the cults, require people to measure up to their gods' will in order to gain their acceptance. God's grace is another reason why I believe that God had to have inspired the Bible and that it isn't the product of the human mind, because the whole Bible presents that divine, non-human trait."

Holly said, "The need to measure up is the message I got in the Catholic church and school."

Joe responded, "It's really unbelievable that God—if he does exist—would just accept me with his no-strings-attached grace! How can he act that way?"

I intoned to both of them, "Imagine that your bosses said to you, 'Your work falls far short of my expectations, but I'm going to promote you anyway.' That action would be grace that is unlike most human thinking and living."

Joe intoned, "I'll say! My boss certainly never would have promoted me without my superior performance. He was a perfectionist!"

Holly agreed, "Mine is too."

I sensed God's work in their lives as I continued with even more intensity, "I believe on the basis of the Bible's teaching that God accepts believers just as they are, even though they're far from perfect like David, not due to their goodness but because of Jesus' perfect life and death on the cross in our place!"

Joe protested as he lifted his ample head and pushed his chest out toward me, "I always thought that I could be good enough by being a good person to please God, if he does exist. Now, you're saying that I *can't?!*"

Holly chimed in, "Yeah, what about doing penance for our sins?"

I replied, "Holly, the Bible says that our works, like penance, must always be the result of our faith through the power released by Jesus' resurrection. I saw the human way of honoring people for their performance in sales management. And the same kind of human thinking sometimes, sadly, happens in the church, which should be full of God's grace! But, of course, my experience has been that the church is full of sinners, many of whom have received God's grace but all of whom have the old sinful nature still within them!

"Jesus said, 'Be perfect, therefore, as your heavenly Father is perfect' in his Sermon on the Mount in Matthew 5:48. But it's Jesus' divine perfection by which God the Father accepts imperfect believers! That astounding grace is another reason I believe that God inspired the Bible, because the performance-oriented human mind could never have thought up the concept and power of grace."

Joe, who was eagerly hanging on my every word, asked with a puzzled expression, "Power! What power?"

Holly echoed Joe, "Yeah, Bruce, what power? I don't remember hearing about the power of grace in church."

I answered, "The one only true God of the Bible merely wants people to accept Jesus' perfect life and death in their place and his powerful grace to be rescued from our imperfections. Joe and Holly, if you accept his grace, he'll change you too with his power."

Joe lowered his gaze, "I'm not ready yet. I can't believe the unbelievable."

Holly averted her eyes too, "I'm not so sure either."

My reply came quickly, "I understand. By the way, I've been talking about the 'amazing grace' that the song talks about."

Holly said, "I don't remember hearing much about grace when I was growing up, much less that song."

Joe observed, "O, yeah, I've heard that song at funerals, but doesn't...that idea make...people lazy?"

"No, God's great grace is a power that changes true Christians to *want* to do the things that *he* wants us to do, according to the Bible. That is, he enables us to avoid disobedience and to grow in obedience, sometimes by allowing bad things like our son's death to happen in our lives."

Holly interjected, "Your boy died, Bruce?! What happened?"

I answered her, "Holly, I already told Joe that our second child, Keith, died from leukemia when he was four-and-a-half years old, in my last year of teaching when I was running away from God's call to the ministry and that his death was the means that God used to change my heart to be open to his call to be a preacher. After three years of sales management, God sent me back to school with a wife, three children, and no job. However, he provided for us...."

Holly interrupted, "That's terrible, Bruce. How did you deal with losing your boy?"

"Only by God's grace, Holly. I told Joe that God provided Winnie with his gift of peace when the doctor told us that Keith only had a 50-50 chance to live and me with that same peace fifteen years later after my seven years of depression."

Holly and Joe feel silent.

I resumed my description of believers' victory, "The resulting good of his work in believers' lives is that he enables us to make progress in following his will instead of our selfish wills, an on-going process called sanctification (being made more and more *holy*), that takes a whole lifetime...."

"Sancti-*what*-tion!?" exclaimed Joe.

I smiled at the hot-tub clown, "You might call it '*saint*-ification,' a process by which God gradually makes every believer more and more a *saint*!"

Joe's wry smile suddenly shifted to a serious expression, "I thought that those people did miracles and were only a few really holy people."

Holly interjected, "I was taught the same thing about saints, Joe. I'm far from being a saint."

Joe's eyes bugged out, "You're saying that every believer in your God is a *saint*!?"

My answer brought a broad smile to Joe's face, "I'm a sinner too. However, Paul makes that truth clear by addressing as saints all of the believers in the churches to whom he wrote."

Joe lifted his right hand high in the humid air, "Maybe some day I can be a saint too, and it's a free gift on top of it!"

Holly replied, "I find it really hard to believe that I can become a saint."

"Holly and Joe, I hope you can be saints too. After all, Holly, all you need to do is take away one letter out of your name and believe in Jesus, and you become 'holy' with all other believers as a saint. Holy Holly—that name has a good ring to it," I said grinning.

Joe and Holly chortled at my joke.

I continued, "However, the so-called 'grace' that people accept and that allows them to go on disobeying God without any change in their lives is what Bonhoeffer, a minister who was killed by the Nazis for his belief in the only true God just before World War II ended, called 'cheap grace.' It isn't God's real grace of Ephesians 2:1-10. There Paul writes that God's grace through faith—a personal trust—in Jesus makes us alive from our 'normal' death in sin that started with Adam's sin that made him dead to God. Paul went on to write that God makes us into his 'workmanship'—his work of art—to do good works that he prepared beforehand for us to do. From the time we believe in the true God, we begin following Jesus throughout life instead of Satan!"

Joe looked at me with his eyebrows lifted high and his jaw jutted out, "I find grace hard to believe."

Holly agreed, "Me too."

My eagerness responded, "That grace described in the Bible could never have come from the self-help human minds that started all the other spiritual groups. It's definitely a concept that shows that God inspired the Bible!"

Overwhelmed by deep thought, Joe slowly shook his head and said haltingly, "I just can't *buy* it, Bruce—not yet."

"You can believe or not believe whatever you want, Joe, but you can't *buy* him. You can only *accept* him! God's grace is not hard to accept if you grant me the belief that he is the Creator of all things and people. Also, grant me the belief that he entered a human body to become Jesus in order to do all of those amazing actions perfectly. He performed those miracles to show us God the Father by the Holy Spirit's power. After all, the Bible says that the Apostle John was an eyewitness who was willing to die for his testimony that Jesus' miracles, death, and resurrection were historical facts."

Holly intoned, "I believe in God as Creator of the universe, but I have doubts about Jesus as God, the way the priests and nuns taught me in my youth."

After a pause, a hint of a smile crept across my face as I exclaimed, "Hey, I just thought of something! The 3-in-1 God rescued the three of us from the three Stooges attempting to rob the bank! It was the 3-in-1 Rescuer saving us from three sinners with one purpose!"

Joe replied, "Whoa, slow down, buddy!...I guess you *might* have a point."

Holly said to both of us, "The nuns taught me that God is three Persons in one God, but I'll have to think about that one."

CHAPTER 21

Real permanent change

I returned to our discussion as I leaned forward with my left hand receiving my right fist, "During my whole life as a child and teenager until I was sixteen, I had been an unbeliever like my father, who stayed home from church, while mom 'dragged' us boys to church. Then, God convinced me that he is real, he inspired the Bible, and Jesus is God. How?

"As I told you before, Joe, when I was sixteen my mother changed churches to one that preached those beliefs. After I saw *The Ten Commandments* in the movie theater for the first time in 1957 or 1958—yeah, I'm an old guy!" (Joe and Holly smirked.)—"I was awestruck by God's power depicted by the plagues in Egypt and especially the opening of the Red Sea. The movie showed that last event just the way it is described in the Bible as witnessed by two million Israelites and the Egyptian army.

"Also, when I searched the Bible, the centuries-old prophecies fulfilled by Jesus' birth, many miracles, life, death, and resurrection impressed me. However, the question whether Jesus truly is God boiled down," as I pointed at the bubbling water with a grin, "to the question of whether Jesus *really* rose permanently from the dead, unlike Jesus' miracle of raising Lazarus, who rose temporarily only to die again later."

"Go on, Bruce. What convinced you?" Holly asked me.

"Well, I came to understand the historical fact that the disciples, during their time with Jesus, expected that Jesus would get rid of the Roman occupiers of Palestine and set up an earthly kingdom. Then, his followers would be the rulers under Jesus with power and prestige. Similarly, God's people at that time expected that the Messiah would be an earthly ruler.

"However, when the Roman soldiers nailed him to a criminal's cross on a hill outside of Jerusalem, his followers' earthly hopes of future fame and fortune failed. On the other hand, three days after Jesus' death, an event happened in their lives that changed their gloom into lasting joy and their discouragement into courage. They emerged from the upper room in Jerusalem to proclaim that they had seen Jesus alive from the dead!"

Joe said as he and Holly leaned forward, "Go on, Bruce."

"That historical fact, which his eyewitnesses recorded at least five times in the Bible and for which Jesus' followers were willing to *suffer* and *die*, happened as a historical event, I reasoned. If you and I had made up such a fantastic tale or merely imagined it, we would have admitted our falsehood or flight of fancy at the first sign of opposition. Well, they experienced not only one but three kinds of persecution from the Jews, Greeks, and Romans! God, therefore, convinced me that Jesus indeed rose from the dead because of his courageous eyewitnesses, not one of whom denied their story. His resurrection must be a historical fact.

"It was those same testimonies that his followers wrote down at God's leading for us to read in the Bible. Therefore, I came to the conclusion that since Jesus really came back to permanent life, God *has* to be real and, in addition, really did inspire the Bible. It's that same God who is progressively transforming my life from disobedience like that of Adam to obedience like that of Jesus. However, I have a long way to go!"

Joe's skepticism showed up, "But what about all those translations and manuscripts during the 2,000 years since the Bible was written? How do you know which is the *real* Bible?"

CHAPTER 22

A mysterious God revealed

    I prayerfully parried the sword of Joe's doubt with soft sounds, "Joe, I'm glad that you asked that question. Through study, I discovered that the trail of manuscripts goes all the way back to the third and fourth centuries, with a few fragments from only two decades after the Bible was written. By contrast, other ancient manuscripts have the closest, available copies to the original writings as old as a whole millenium after Plato's *Republic*, for example. When the King James Bible's translation was copied, the available manuscripts were copies made a 1,000 years after Christ.

    "However, during the next 450 years after the King James Bible was translated, people discovered more ancient manuscripts of the Bible. Those discovered copies bring us much closer to the original writings. However, the differences between the King James manuscripts and those earlier manuscripts from which the *New International Version* was translated are unimportant in terms of the Bible's message.

    "All scholars agree that the King James Bible is about 95% like the original writings, and the NIV Bible that I gave you, Joe, is 99.9%+ like the original eyewitnesses' writings. The Bible is by far the best preserved ancient manuscript. You can be sure that, as you read the NIV, you are reading a faithful translation of the original Bible. Holly, do you have an up-to-date version of the Bible to read?"

    "No, when I was growing up, we didn't have our own Bibles. The priests were the authorities who interpreted the Bible for us."

    I asked her as I sat on the hot-tub's edge, "Would you like to have one? I can give you a Bible the way I did for Joe."

    "I sure would!"

    Joe interjected, "But what about all of the various interpretations of the Bible by Christian denominations? Who are we to believe?"

Unfazed by Joe's hot-tub inquiries, I honored his question, "Well, Joe, you ask a hard question. The Christian denominations came about because of different cultures, sin, and human personalities, not because God wanted it that way. You see, the church is full of imperfect sinners, even though many of them are believing sinner-saints rescued by God's grace. Different cultures in different countries produced different churches. But *all* of the truly-Christian denominations and churches, Catholics and Protestants alike—not the cults—agree on the basic beliefs about which I've been telling you, especially that God is the 3-in-1 Creator and Rescuer who inspired the Bible to reveal himself to us and that Jesus is the God-man."

"There's that 3-in-1-God thing," Joe stated with a big frown.

"Yes, Joe. All illustrations of God's 3-in-1 nature break down because God's nature is really different from anything in the world. However, it might help you to think that God is a *tiny* bit like an egg with its three parts: the shell like the Holy Spirit, the white like God the Father, and the yolk like Jesus. Yet he is very different because he is mysteriously *one* God, not three gods. On the other hand, you might compare him to a peanut covered by chocolate and candy...."

Joe interrupted, "Now, you're talkin'!"

Holly agreed, "Yeah, that's the ticket. I'm a chocoholic."

Joe and I responded together, "I am too!"

"However, all earthly comparisons break down completely in the end," I continued.

Joe grinned, "I know why you believe that God inspired the Bible, as you've said before, 'because the human mind couldn't have thought him up,' right?"

"Right!"

Joe suddenly shot his words at me like sarcastic slingshot stones, "But, Bruce, those are only fictitious stories!" At the exact end of Joe's skeptical sentence and before I could ward off his stinging but friendly attack, Joe clutched at his ample, bare chest; winced at sudden, severe, seering pain; and fell backward with a soft thud.

CHAPTER 23

A Mysterious Disappearance

The lifeguard on duty, a thin young man in his early twenties, rushed to Joe's aid. The called paramedics hurried him to the local hospital, where tests again revealed that Joe's heart was good and that there was no physical cause for his symptoms. He told Holly and me that puzzling fact as we parted that night.

The next afternoon I stopped at the hospital to visit Joe on my way to the pool. The young woman with blond hair and silky skin at the front desk said that Joe was no longer there but that she didn't know where he went after he checked out.

After a Joe-less time at the swimming pool, I placed a quick call to his parents' house, which was answered by his mother, "Hello, Smith residence."

"Hi, Josephine, this is Bruce. I missed Joe at the pool. What happened to him? He didn't have another accident, did he?"

"No, he didn't. He went away for awhile and will be back in a few weeks. He said to tell you and Holly not to worry about him, but he didn't want anyone to know where he went."

"Well, thanks, Josephine," I mumbled, dumbfounded at Joe's mysterious disappearance.

CHAPTER 24

Joe's revelation

After four weeks of anxious, impatient waiting, Holly and I were lounging in the swimming-pool hot-tub when Joe entered from the men's locker room with a languid limp, dove into the pool at the deep end, and swam many laps with his characteristic crawl. We waited for him by fidgeting and teetering on the hot-tub's edge. Joe finally emerged energetically with his characteristic limp from the shallow end of the pool as the late-afternoon sun shone effervesantly on the Joe-disturbed surface of the water.

He slipped into the hot-tub on the west side away from his usual spot in the northeast corner, even though there was no one else besides Holly and me in the steamy, roiling water. He greeted us with an upbeat tone, "Hey, Bruce and Holly, how's it goin'?"

I returned his friendly, joyful tone, "OK, Joe. How's it goin' with *you*? I was worried about you 'cause of your sudden, mysterious disappearance."

Holly echoed me, "Yeah, Joe, I was worried too."

He lowered his voice, "I was at Pine Rest in Grand Rapids, Michigan, where you were a patient. Boy, they sure teach a patient a lot about anger and stuff. My time there was hardly a rest in the pines!"

My tense muscles suddenly relaxed, "Yeah, they try to help your emotions, reasoning, *and* decisions. What did you learn about yourself, Joe?"

"I learned that I'm depressed about Jean's death, my childhood, my car accident, and the bank robbery. I'm on medication to relieve the symptoms of depression and to prevent my anxiety attacks."

Holly stated, "I'm happy that you got help for your depression and anxiety attacks, Joe. That attack in this hot-tub was scary."

I responded, "I'm glad that you discovered those facts about yourself. As I've shared with you, I was an angry, anxious man when I was a patient at Pine Rest without recognizing those emotions. When I met with my therapist there, I shared with him my anger about a seemingly-unimportant incident with my older brother when I must have been four or five years old. He and his friends were having a good time in his treehouse only a few feet above the ground in one of our backyard trees, when I knocked on the makeshift door. Because he and his friends were six years older than I was, they told me to 'get lost.' But when I continued to knock, they emerged down the short ladder and surrounded me to chant, 'Look at the little cry-baby!'

"My therapist, a middle-aged, balding man, suddenly stopped me with his request, 'Bruce, close your eyes and imagine that scene.' As I did, he said, 'Imagine that Jesus comes into that scene. What does he do?' In my imagination, I saw Jesus in his flowing white robe coming to all of us, balling out my brother and his friends, and then hugging *all* of us!

"At that point I shrank from him in my imagination! I didn't want him to hug all of us. I just wanted him to hug me! My therapist said that I had experienced a miracle, because Jesus did the unexpected thing by showing his grace to all of us. That experience showed me that Jesus loves me and confirmed to me again that God inspired the Bible, because it shows his unexpected grace!"

With his eyes and mouth wide open, Joe said, "You sure have had a lot of unusual experiences, Bruce. They had a chaplain at Pine Rest who tried to share God with me. However, I told him that I already have a minister doing that back here and that I didn't want to have more than one ganging up on me. If God does exist, he seems to have pursued me all the way to Pine Rest!"

"So, how was your experience at Pine Rest?" I asked.

CHAPTER 25

An Explanation of Evil

Joe said with his hands splashing into the water, "Not as dramatic as yours. They uncovered the roots of my depression and helped me understand it. By and large, it was a good experience."

"Well, I'm glad, Joe!...How's your reading going?"

"I've finished the Gospel of John, but I still can't accept your belief that God—if he does exist—inspired the Bible. Look at all of the bad things going on in the world. There are car bombings, 9-11, horrible disasters, and now America's financial meltdown! How could your God have let all of those things happen, if he's a loving God?"

Holly chimed in, "That's a good question, Joe. How can God allow all of those things to happen, Bruce?"

My heartfelt reply was quick, "Joe and Holly, I believe that God is loving, but he's also a just God, according to the Bible, his Book. He's your Creator and has every right in the universe to expect the human race to obey him as their Creator, the way the Bible says. Because humans decide to ignore him, go their own way, and refuse to follow his ways of love, he lets them have their own way, even if it means that their greed creates financial havoc. The Bible also says that the human race's rebellion affected God's universe so that earthquakes and bad storms are the result. We have gotten ourselves into our own messes with our self-centeredness. However, there will come a day when Jesus returns and judges all of us with his perfect justice.

"In the meantime he allows those horrible things to happen in order to call everyone back to him. The wonderful good news of the Bible is that if we accept Jesus as our substitute by receiving God the Father's grace, then he makes us right with him now and will declare us 'not guilty' at his Final Judgment. However, it's also a sad truth that rejection means disaster. In addition, the persistent sin of human rebellion isn't God's fault."

Joe and Holly's ensuing silence made me guess that God was making some progress with them. We parted with a decision that we would watch a Cubs' playoff game together the following Wednesday night in my basement surround-sound room.

* * *

"The grass withers and the flowers fall, because the breath of the LORD blows on them. Surely the people are grass. The grass withers and the flowers fall, but the word of our God endures forever."
(Isaiah 40:7, 8)

Part Four Questions:

1. In what ways is the narrator's comment, "It's a great day to be alive...," to which Joe agrees, a foreshadowing of events later in the chapter? How much do you agree with that statement?
2. How do you feel about Joe's objections to and the narrator's answers about the seriousness of sin?
3. What do you think about the narrator's contrast between a cleanly homemaker and God's cleansing of our sins? How can we be justified (declared right by God)? Cleansed from our sins?
4. How do you respond to the narrator's definition of sin? How did Joe respond?
5. What do you think about the narrator's distinction between people-pleasing and ready-rebellion, both of which are sin? What is the biblical definition of sin? How are people compared to dogs and cats? How valid is that comparison?
6. How often do people do the double blame game of Adam and Eve about their sins? How valid is it to blame others for your sins? Why or why not?
7. How often do people think of God as their "great Santa in the sky," as Joe says? How is God different from the usual myth of Santa Claus? What is the best way to teach our children the truth about Santa and the true God?
8. What are your reactions to the bank-robbery scene? How does that event affect the friendship of Joe and the narrator? How does it relate to their discussion about sin?
9. At the end of this part, what idea, repeated several times so far, does the narrator share with Joe? How valid is that idea about God and the Bible, in your estimation?

PART 5

How can God be our Father?

CHAPTER 26

A deep, dark secret

On the following Wednesday night, after a cloudy, windy, dark day—Holly, Joe, and I enjoyed one another's company in my W'nW (watching and writing) room, even though the Cubs lost their first playoff game to the Dodgers. After the game ended and we had commiserated about their loss, I retrieved a Bible for Holly, as I had promised her, and asked Joe, "How are you doing, Joe—really?"

"Well, I'm looking for a job, Bruce. I heard once that looking for a job is a full-time job."

"I'm glad that you've decided to take that step. Something that I've wondered about since we last talked is what you said about your childhood. At Pine Rest I first recognized my anger at an emotionally-distant, dysfunctional family and my permissive, traveling-salesman Dad, who was gone all week. As a result, I was angry that I was stuck with my overly-strict Mom, the daughter of my grandpa, the county judge. That situation was almost unbearable, especially in the summer, when we gardened organically the *lo-o-ong* way by hand, before organic gardening was in vogue. Her garden was at least 100 square miles large, it seemed to me."

Both Joe, seated on the blue, over-stuffed couch to my right, and Holly, on the matching love seat to my left, let out a hearty chuckle. After a pause Joe lowered his voice and edged from the blue couch to within inches of my recliner by grabbing a folding chair and plopping down with a soft thud. He looked at Holly and then at me, "Bruce and Holly, can you keep a secret to prevent vicious gossip?" In immediate response to our emphatically-nodding heads, he whispered with the veins bulging in his forehead, "My dad *liked* little boys when I was young, if you know what I mean."

My eyes bulged out as my mouth widened, "That's horrible, Joe!"

"O no, Joe!" Holly exclaimed.

"He also liked little girls!" Joe confided with tears welling up in his eyes. "My mother knew about it but did nothing! Of course, our small-town reputation had to be protected at *all* costs. The people at Pine Rest helped me remember those revolting experiences, and I've been grieving ever since my stay there. As they said, it's important to face and deal with traumatic experiences rather than bury them inside us with the possible results of depression and anxiety attacks. You said that too. My sister and I plan to confront our parents, as I practiced in psychodrama."

Joe straightened up as if a great weight was lifted from his shoulders and asked me, while surprisingly shifting gears, "What else did you discover about *your* childhood, Bruce?"

I whispered as if we were three pirate friends getting away with a heist, "My parents, who have both died, were 'divorced' within marriage. They lived in two separate worlds and favored my two brothers. They never agreed on how to discipline us boys. As a result, I was very insecure. Since bullies on the school playground sensed my insecurity, they picked on me. For example, they dragged me out to the snowball field in the winter to pelt me with snowballs there.

"I'll never forget the evening that Dad threatened divorce. Mom was an idealistic environmentalist in the 1950s, while Dad was a practical farmer at heart. He wanted to put tile in the field's swamp to get a few more acres of crops, while Mom opposed his plan in order to save the swamp creatures. One evening they argued at the top of their lungs in the living room, while my younger brother and I cowered in the hallway. Then, Dad yelled, 'If you don't let me tile the swamp, I will divorce you and leave!' My brother and I looked at each other in panic. Mom's prolonged silence ended their argument. Dad then tiled the swamp. I've been thankful ever since then that Mom backed down, because Dad and I shared TV together."

Holly said, "You had a tough childhood."

Grateful for Holly's empathy, I said, "Years later when I was 43 years old, I grieved out that whole, abnormal situation in prayer until God gave me peace. In addition, the enormous good that God brought out of that unhealthy family situation when I was 16 was that Jesus filled up my loneliness and insecurity. Thus, he overcame my confused isolation! He's promised in the Bible that he will always overcome evil for believers' good. That promise fulfilled in my life is another reason that I believe Jesus is God."

Puzzled Joe asked, "How can you say that Jesus came into your life? If he is alive—as you say he is—hasn't he gone to heaven? How can he be here and there at the same time?"

I asserted to both of them, "His virgin birth by way of the Holy Spirit overshadowing the virgin Mary, his many miracles, his forgiveness of the people who crucified him, his resurrection from the dead, his offer of the Father's rescue to everyone who would accept him, and his return to heaven—his followers witnessed all of those events—are actions that demonstrate to me that he is God, who is present everywhere throughout his creation. At the same time, it's true that he also has a human body that his followers touched after he arose from the dead. He used that same resurrected body, then, to eat broiled fish in the eyewitnesses' presence. His miraculous body is also now in heaven with his heavenly Father, who is also everywhere in his creation."

"The Bible sure tells some whoppers," Joe said with a frown and clenched fists.

I grinned, "They aren't whoppers. You can only get those at a fast-food restaurant and in worship groups that make us powerful people in our own strength. There are no fictional stories in the Bible, Joe."

Joe's reply was his grinning silence until he said slowly, as his face relapsed into a deep frown, "I...have trouble with...the idea of a heavenly...Father, since my father abused me."

Holly looked at Joe, "I also have that problem, since my father disciplined us kids too severely and arbitrarily with a strap."

CHAPTER 27

A perfect Father

"I can understand why you're both hesitant, but God the Father is very different from our imperfect earthly fathers. He is loving and yet just, close to us and yet far away, and angry at our sins as well as fully-forgiving when we trust in Jesus. He is the *perfect* Father who himself provided the loving solution. He gave his only beloved Son to die in our place. On the other hand, our fathers are very *imperfect* because of the human race's fall into sin."

Joe fixed his gaze on me, "I've always wondered, Bruce, about the teaching that Jesus died in my place. If I'm guilty because of my imperfections and worthy of death, as I read in Genesis chapter three about Adam as the head of humans, how can Jesus pay for that penalty?"

"Well, my understanding of the Bible is that Jesus, God the Father, and the Spirit came up with that plan. Someone leading a perfect life has to pay for everyone's guilt and to take the death penalty for our disobedience. Like an earthly judge, God exacts punishment for sin. We can't pay the penalty ourselves because we are far from perfect. If you will read further in the Old Testament, you will see that God's rules for Israel involved the slaughter of animals that had to be blemish-free.

"God the Father knew before he created Adam and Eve that they would disobey him. However, their disobedience was not at all his fault. He and the second Person of God, who later became Jesus, both perfectly planned to sacrifice Jesus as our perfect Substitute and Solution. As a result, he died a cruel and painful death on a criminal's cross outside of Jerusalem. Joe and Holly, did you ever hear Jesus being referred as the Lamb of God?"

Joe pinched his face and closed his eyes, "Yeah, I remember some of the songs in Sunday School using that name. I have often wondered why they called Jesus a Lamb."

Holly agreed, "I remember some of the Catholic liturgy talking about Jesus as the Lamb. I vaguely recall that John the Baptist called Jesus the Lamb of God."

My reply was rapid-fire, "That's right, Holly. The background is that the Passover lamb, which each family had to slaughter once a year at the place of worship, gave its blood. At the first Passover celebration in Egypt before their escape from slavery, the people smeared that lamb's blood on their doors so that the angel that destroyed all of the firstborn sons of rebellious Egypt would *pass over* their houses. Similarly, God provided Jesus as his Lamb, the Substitute, for us who believe in him. The result is that our right verdict of 'guilty' with our death penalty and our separation from God both change to the Judge's verdict 'not guilty' resulting in life forever with him.

"Thus, he opened the way for believers to talk to him all the time as his friends rather than being his non-communicating enemies, which I was for the first sixteen years of my life. God then becomes our Father."

Joe's response was muffled as he sat on that rickety folding chair a few inches from my recliner, "That idea is beyond my experience. However, I can't accept him as my Father—not yet!"

Holly nodded, "I'll think about your explanation, Bruce."

My reply was equally muffled, "I understand. At Pine Rest the staff took me off of all medications to observe my symptoms. And I've never been back on meds to control my depression or anxiety attacks, not one of which has returned. Furthermore, God has given me grace to forgive him for allowing bad events in my life. He also gave me the power to forgive my family and others who have sinned against me. It's all to the 3-in-1 God's credit!"

Joe inquired, "Why aren't you on meds for depression and anxiety attacks the way I am, Bruce?"

Holly echoed Joe, "You're not on medications, Bruce?"

CHAPTER 28

Real peace

I responded as I leaned forward in my recliner, "Well, the chaplain gave me a book about anger. I read one chapter a night until the twelfth night, when I read the chapter entitled, 'Anger at God.' I didn't finish reading it that night because I felt I had to pray instead, as my tears gushed down my cheeks, 'Dear God—Father, Jesus, and Holy Spirit— one only true God, I praise you for sending me here to Pine Rest to get in touch with my anger about the past. However, I'm very angry at some people for their sins against me and also at you, dear God, for allowing me to be born into a dysfunctional family, permitting my brother Bobby to die from leukemia when I was two and a half months old, allowing people to do un-Christian things to me, and allowing Keith to die from leukemia.

"'At the same time, Father, I confess my self-centered sins in wanting *my* plan instead of *your* plan for my life. Because my grief has been a heavy burden for me to carry, my bitterness has been an emotional barrier between you and me during the 43 years of my life. Forgive me for my self-centered sins in questioning your permissive plan and lift my heavy burden of angry grief. Lord, give me peace about the past! Through Jesus alone, amen!'

"Joe and Holly, Jesus gave me the outlet of many tears and prayers to him as he came close to me, so that after I prayed three or four times a week for seven and a half months, my depression left. After another month of prayers, he gave me the peace that transcends understanding, which Philippians 4:6,7 describes as God's response to our persistent prayers. At that point my anger about the past was gone, my yielding to his plan was complete, and my depression has never returned! God changed me through those prayers, tears, and confession without changing the past. I continue to use those lamenting prayers every time my stress builds up! It's because of that experience of God's peace that's beyond human understanding that I'm firmly convinced that Jesus has worked in my life so amazingly."

Joe objected, "That's an amazing story, Bruce, but I can't accept God as a Father who allows such terrible tragedies in his plan for a person's life. Your brother died from leukemia as well as your son?! How could God, if he does exist, allow both of those things to happen to the same person?"

My reply blurted out, "Joe, God definitely didn't *cause* those things to happen. He only *allowed* them to happen for me to learn his loving lessons. It seems to me that God brought good out of Bobby's death, as his Word promises to all believers in tough times, by teaching me sixteen years later to seek his strength humbly instead of depending on myself. Also, he used Keith's death to bring me closer to him and to change my heart to seek his will for my vocational choice when I was rebelling against his call to be a pastor. The upshot was that God renewed his call to the ministry from which I had rebelled at college because I would have had to climb the 'Mount Everest' of a Greek major in order to enter seminary.

"However, he also permitted me to experience severe, tingling, stabbing pain in my feet and hands that started the morning of the fourth Friday of March, 1986, at the depth of my depression, about the time that I experienced two severe anxiety attacks like yours. At Mayo Clinic several years later, I discovered that a rare hereditary nerve disease had been amplifying my pain and is slowly but surely taking over my legs with numbness. Much more recently, an MRI in Cedar Rapids showed that my leg and foot pain is the result of two pinches in my lower back. I see a spine surgeon there next week for his opinion about possible surgery."

CHAPTER 29

Coping with pain

Joe's and Holly's mouths dropped as I spoke about my pain, and Joe barely managed to mouth his next words, "How can you...cope with having...pain all the time?"

"Well, almost thirteen years after the pain started, in the winter of 1999, I was getting a little tired again. As a result, I asked God why I was getting depressed. The thought came to me that I was depressed about the pain. It took two months of nightly laments expressing my anger at God for allowing, not causing, the pain and confessing my selfishness in wanting a pain-free life. At the end of that lamenting time, God again gave me his permanent peace about that issue. *The* pain became *my* pain. God set me free of the heavy burden of anger about my pain forever!

"That's amazing, Bruce!" Holly exclaimed.

"God also gave me more ways to control my pain and further understanding of the good things that he has brought out of my pain. Jesus, my personal God-man, healed me of my anger about that issue! He also enables me to be in constant prayer and keeps me humbly dependent on him because of my pain. Maybe some day I'll write a book entitled *God Is My Shrink*! a variation on the title of the 1945 film *God Is My Co-Pilot*. It's a true story in which a World War 2 pilot goes after Japanese pilots who killed his pilot buddy. Of course, my title would refer to God as my constant Psychiatrist, who shrinks my doubts down to nothing. It will also be a satire of the American idea that we can drag God into our lives as an emergency-squad god like a co-pilot and nothing more. He firmly refuses to be treated like a part-time God."

Joe expressed his wonder, "Is there never an end to the amazing things that have happened to you, Bruce? I just wish I could have your kind of faith."

"Both of you can by trusting in Jesus as your God-man, who died and rose again to rescue you personally from the death penalty of sin, and commit your lives to him. At the same time, you can believe in the 3-in-1 God as the one, only true God, who made you and came into the world in Jesus to rescue you." I leaned forward with a preacher's hand-waving.

Joe's skepticism arose, "Bruce, it's all too unbelievable!"

Holly shook her head, "How could God allow my own father's stern, unloving actions?"

"I don't know, Holly. Maybe some day you both can accept God as your perfect, loving Father," I intoned with a slight frown.

"Yeah, maybe some day," Joe replied with a little grin as Holly nodded slowly with a frown.

* * *

"For in Christ all the fullness of the Deity lives in bodily form, and in Christ you have been brought to fullness. He is the head over every power and authority."

(Colossians 2:9,10)

* * *

Part Five Questions:

1. Which of Joe's objections is the strongest one in challenging our faith in God's inspiration of the Bible? How did the narrator answer it? What other answers could be made?
2. What doubts do you have about the Bible's inspiration? How can those doubts be answered?
3. When does doubt help us grow in our faith? When is it harmful to our faith?
4. What does the narrator mean by God's "inspiration" of the Bible? How adequate is that explanation?
5. Why do the narrator and Joe agree that the argument that Jesus was only a good teacher is wrong? What two choices does a person have when confronted with Jesus' claims that he was God? How does the narrator support his choice that Jesus is actually God? What does that choice have to do with the Bible's inspiration?
6. Define grace. What does its presence in the Bible have to do with the Bible's inspiration? How does the narrator explain the power of God's grace as opposed to "cheap grace"? How do you feel about God's grace given to you through Jesus?
7. Why does Joe say, "I can't believe the unbelievable"? How does the narrator respond? How would you have responded? Why?
8. What comparison between the bank robbery and God does the narrator suddenly make? How effective is his testimony about his own conversion? Why?
9. What other objections and answers about God's inspiration of the Bible happen? How effectively does the narrator answer Joe's objections and questions? How did this discussion affect your faith?
10. What further objections did Joe have to believing in God after his mysterious disappearance and re-appearance? How does the narrator answer those objections? How do the narrator's experiences when he was in therapy help your faith?

PART 6:

Is God Just?

CHAPTER 30

An arrest

Holly, Joe, and I decided to go golfing on the following Saturday at the golf course where we had golfed in May one more time before the weather turned cold. It was another dark and cloudy day made even darker by the Dodgers' playoff sweep of our Cubs. I again picked up Joe and Holly in my Pontiac Vibe to plumb the depths of horrible hooks (balls that curve to the left) and sandy slices (the other way). As Joe slouched into the front seat, his dark mood matched the continuing weather.

"What's the matter, Joe?"

"Have you heard the bad news? Not only have the Cubs bombed out again, but my father has been arrested for having his way with a nine-year-old boy. I'm afraid that the whole mess will make our town his judge and jury long before the trial! You know what small towns are like." A tear traced down his cheek.

Holly exclaimed from the back seat, "That's terrible news, Joe! Were you and Phyllis able to confront him with his sexual abuse?"

"No, we were going to get together with him this week, and now the police are involved," Joe droned in a monotone.

Feeling helpless, I asked, leaning forward as I drove and glanced at Joe, "Is there anything I can do?"

Joe heaved a long sigh, "I don't know what you can do."

We arrived at the golf course's hilly links, went through the motions of mediocre swings, and finished with nothing more than three hours of good exercise, as we grieved mutually over the Cubs and the predicament that Joe's father, Phil, had brought on himself and his family. I broke our silence that had lasted a few holes on the ninth fairway with a question and a suggestion to Joe, "Is Phil in jail or at home? Maybe I can visit him as a friend of the family."

"He's still in jail. Would you, Bruce? That would be great!"

Holly agreed, "A visit might be just the ticket for Phil."

CHAPTER 31

A bleak visit

The steel door of Phil's jail cell clanked coldly shut as I edged into the tight, dark room. Phil was seated on the far end of his bunk as I plunked my body noisily on the near end. "How are you doing, Phil?" came my usual question, which suddenly seemed out of place in that dingy dungeon.

Phil, a squatty, sullen, balding, sixty-year-old man, answered with bulging veins on his forehead, "How do you suppose I am?!...I'm sorry; I shouldn't take my predicament out on you...," as his high-pitched voice trailed off to a mere squeak. Recovering somewhat, he managed with a frown, "I just don't want any God-talk, Bruce."

"Fair enough, Phil," I suddenly saw the source of his son's skepticism. "What happened to end you up in here, from your point-of-view?"

"Well, yesterday at noon I was minding my own business when the cops showed up at my house, handcuffed me, and dragged me to this God-forsaken jail! They didn't even offer me one phone call!" His seething rage suddenly boiled as he slammed his coiled fist against one of the upright boards of the roughly-carpentered bunk and then shook it despairingly. "I'm afraid you wasted a trip here, Bruce. I haven't darkened the door of a church in years. Phyllis has been the church-goer, dragging our kids there."

"Phil, what kind of injustice do you see here?"

He leaned back against a wooden cross-slat. "O, it's that kid next-door. I've asked him several times to stop playing ball in the street with our house in 'left field.' I told him that some day he and his friends would break a window in our house. Well, yesterday my prediction came true! I yelled at him, and he sneaked home with a stupid story that I had played around with him. What a bunch of crock! Now, the whole town will gossip viciously...as if I'm guilty...when I'm not!"

I was at a loss for words as I sat there wishing that I was somewhere else—anywhere! Phil rambled on righteously as he justified himself, until he also ran out of words. Then I asked, "Is there anything I can do for you, Phil?"

He replied with a hoarse raspiness and pursed eyebrows, "No, your God can't help me!" I secretly, silently hoped and prayed that Phil's helplessness and hopelessness didn't continue.

Then, the massive iron doors clanked shut ominously behind me. On my way out of our small-town jail, my most fervent prayer was that Joe would overcome his father's source of unbelief.

CHAPTER 32

Miracles?

The next day in the locker room while I was getting undressed, in slouched Joe, whose face brightened when he saw me. "Did you see my father, Bruce?"

"Yeah, I saw him. He claims innocence, Joe."

"He might be innocent with the neighbor boy, but he's guilty with Phyllis and me! Thanks for seeing him!"

"You're welcome! In situations like this one, God comforts me with the truth in his Word that God is the divine Judge who will judge people's sins when Jesus returns. That future event shows me not to judge wrong-doers in this life....Say, Joe, you don't have to hold onto unbelief about God the way your father does. We *can* be different from our fathers. In fact, I imagine that you want to be *very* different from *your* father!"

"I do, Bruce," Joe replied as he faced the concrete floor. However, then he turned to face me, "Say, Bruce, after I finished the Book of John, I decided to go back to Exodus. There, I have just read about the slavery that the Israelites experienced in Egypt. I have heard in the past that those plagues were normal to Egypt and that the 'Red Sea' was only a reedy lake that they waded across. What do you think about those ideas?"

"Yeah, I've heard those same skeptical ideas. Those people's treatment of the Bible assumes that there is nothing miraculous, an unbiblical approach. However, I come to the Bible with the biblical idea that it's God's Word, which assumes that God does miracles. Practically speaking, I believe that God guided the writers to show us the truth. I believe that the interpreters to whom you refer impose the assumptions of science on the Bible.

"Instead, I interpret the Bible from God's own assumptions within the Bible. For example, the Bible assumes that God, the Creator, invaded history to do his miraculous actions, especially at the beginnings of eras like both of the beginnings of Israel as a nation and the Christian church later. Therefore, I interpret the Bible on its own assumptions about God and his people revealed there, since God inspired all of that book.

"I believe that the miracles of the plagues had to do more with the *great* intensity and *exact* timing of those horrible plagues, not that those were brand-new events. Notice that in some of the plagues, Pharoah himself called the shots by asking that the plagues be stopped at a certain time!

"Also, the text, which I believe to be inspired and which the rest of the Bible assumes to be true, says that the later plagues only bothered the Egyptians in the southern part of Egypt, not the Israelites in the northern Nile delta. God's protection of Israel alone was also miraculous.

"As for the opening of the Red Sea, I believe that God—the Creator—Father; the Person of God that later became Jesus, who more than likely was in the pillar of fire and probably in Moses' burning bush; and the Holy Spirit did the miracle. That one, only true God opened the deep water of the Red Sea, piled it up in walls, and made a path of dry dirt on which the Israelites hurried to the other side. Why couldn't he? Not only were there two million Israelites, including Moses, as eyewitnesses, but that miracle was *nothing* for the Creator of the universe. Why do people doubt that the only true, all-powerful Creator could create such a mighty miracle as well as the plagues?

"After all, he made everything. The rest of the Bible assumes that Moses' eyewitness account is literally true as part of Israel's history, because it was Israel's escape (or exodus) from Egypt that was celebrated by the Jewish Passover for 3,500 years."

CHAPTER 33

Human assumptions

The grin on Joe's face showed me that my excitement affected him. Then, he tried to slow me down as he pulled on imaginary reins, "Whoa, there, preacher-man! What do you say about the 'Sea of Reeds,' the description that the footnotes in that Bible that *you* gave me call the Red Sea?"

I grinned broadly, "Tsk, Tsk, Joe, you shouldn't read footnotes. Well, there *is* a reference in 1 Kings 9:26 about Solomon's ship-building at Ezion Geber on the 'Red Sea,' a seaside town bordering the other finger of the real Red Sea on the other side of the Sinai Peninsula, showing that the 'Sea of Reeds' has to be a term for the Red Sea. Also, in Numbers 21:5 (Moses' own description), he writes that, forty years later, Israel walked on a road leading to the Red Sea from Edom, a country near the Dead Sea and not far from the eastern finger of the real Red Sea, which again can't be the shallow Sea of Reeds near Egypt.

"It seems to me that when we assume that there can be no miracles, we go to any lengths to explain them away. Therefore, I disagree with the NIV's footnotes that say it is really the shallow Sea of Reeds near Egypt instead of the Red Sea. After all, the water stood up in walls with water from the Red Sea, as described by Moses and the Psalms," I said as I leaned back against my half-locker on the locker room's stark, sturdy bench and took a deep, satisfied, relaxing breath.

"Well, I just don't buy it!"

"We can agree to disagree, can't we, Joe?" I asked as I eyeballed the echoing locker-room ceiling. In response to Joe's nodding head, I then took that opportunity to advise Joe, "When you get to all of those laws in Exodus, Leviticus, Numbers, and Deuteronomy, please notice that the law of the Ten Commandments in Exodus chapter twenty is introduced by God's words in verses two and three with his own voice from the fiery, cloudy pillar. That pillar probably contained the second Person of God, who later became Jesus Christ. The cloud had descended powerfully on Mount Sinai before God said, 'I am the LORD your God who brought you out of Egypt, out of the land of slavery. You shall have no other gods before me.'

"On the basis of the Bible's teachings, I believe that we are born slaves to sin and to other gods, especially to our egos as the gods with which we were born. However, the God-man Jesus, God the Father's perfect Lamb, releases us through his Passover death by the Holy Spirit's power, from that slavery, when we trust in him. The result, then, is naturally our thankful obedience as his adopted children. The God-man, Jesus, rescues us who believe in him through his death so that we may live a life of free, joyful thankfulness as we follow God's commandments. The same was true for the Israelites, who were called to live thankful, loving lives in response to God's deliverance through the Red Sea."

Joe plunged in, "Wait a minute! I always thought that my good life gets me points with God to go to heaven—if God exists. Instead, you're saying that God would rescue me by his grace and that my thankful life would be the result?!"

"That's right, Joe! I believe what God inspired Paul to write in Ephesians 2:1-10. The Bible's teaching in those words is that we are born dead to God, that *he* makes us alive to him freely, resulting in our personal trust in Jesus by his grace, and that we become his re-made people to do good works that he has prepared for us to do. Our good life is the 'fruit,' not the 'root,' of the 'tree' of God's rescue. The God-man Jesus' grace as his free gift is the 'trunk' of that 'tree,' so to speak!

"Christianity is the only spiritual approach that doesn't require a set of good actions that curry God's love in order for us to receive eternal life. That gift comes to us freely instead. That unique idea shows that Jesus revealed the true God of grace to us in human form because the human race, shown by all of the other religions and the cults, wants to earn God's rescue instead, because they want at least part of the credit. They do not simply want to accept the God-man as the Father's free gift to us!" My upper body leaned toward Joe.

His answering, thoughtful silence accompanied us the rest of the way to the rectangular, slippery cavity, the welcoming, warm water of which waited for our conquering victory once again. Before we enthusiastically skimmed over the frothing depths, I made a suggestion to help Joe's Bible reading, "By the way, Joe, when you're reading through the laws in Exodus through Deuteronomy, I suggest that you get the gist of the repeated laws and go on so that you won't give up or get bogged down because of the repetition."

As we parted outside the exercise facility that afternoon, Holly and Joe wished me well at the surgeon's office the next day.

* * *

> All Scripture is God-breathed and is useful for teaching, rebuking, correcting, and training in righteousness, so that all God's people may be thoroughly equipped for every good work.
> (2 Timothy 3:16,17)

Part Six Questions:

1. What does Joe's revealing of his childhood secret to the narrator say about their relationship? What events to this point have made that relationship grow? How can God develop and grow relationships between us and other people from acquaintance to friendship to fellowship?
2. How would you explain in your own words Jesus' two natures to an unbeliever?
3. How does the sharing between Joe and the narrator about their childhoods help you understand them as characters in the book's plot? How is the fact that Joe shares his secret one turning point in the book? Why?
4. How important are the narrator's words "I understand" in this friendship when Joe expressed his doubts? What other responses would have built walls instead of bridges between the narrator and Joe?
5. How effective is the narrator's explanation of Jesus' payment of the price for our sins? What is your reaction to the narrator's testimony about the good that God brought out of his physical pain? Why?

PART 7

What will happen to us after we die?

CHAPTER 34

Surprising Diagnosis

There are Joe and Bruce already making waves. They tend to do that in my life, in more ways than one. I wonder why they have come into my life. I dive into the deep end and swim my twenty-five minutes until I join the two guys in the hot-spa. I ask Bruce how his appointment with the surgeon went.

"After my uneventful, prayerful trip through rolling farmland to Cedar Rapids, I endured the nurse's many medical questions and waited several minutes for the surgeon. He was a short, stocky man in his mid-forties. After peering at the MRI of my back and examining me, he came right to the point, 'Your situation is a no-brainer! You need surgery on your lumbar region at L4-5. If you agree, my office people will set you up with appointments for the pre-op and surgery.'

"'Let's go for it!' I exclaimed and added, 'What do you think caused the pinches in my spine, doctor?'

"His answer made the rest of my questions fly out of my brain, 'From birth your spinal canal was narrower than normal, a condition called stenosis. As a result, your spine was ready for arthritic-pinches-on-the-nerve to happen. It was an event that more than likely began twenty-three years ago, when your foot pain started.' Stunned silent prayers for successful surgery accompanied my drive home."

Bruce seems to be sincere.

Joe asks, "How can that kind of break-down in the spine happen, Bruce, when you say that your God created the human body?"

"God made Adam and Eve's bodies perfect, Joe, but one result of their rebellion was imperfect bodies like those of all humans. It's the human race's fault, not God's, that bodies get cancer or, in my case, a narrow spine and arthritis. He allowed it to happen but didn't cause it. However, some day when Jesus returns, all believers' bodies will be perfect in resurrection power. Then believers will live forever with him in the new heaven and new earth."

Bruce has many good-sounding answers, but I'm still not ready to accept his ideas as truth. I still feel alienated from all spiritual leaders.

"Bruce, you describe so many unbelievable events!" Joe observes.

He replies, "Well, the Bible promises that my risen body will be like Jesus' risen body! I believe those promises because he definitely rose from the dead, according to many eyewitnesses. I *yearn* for the fulfillment of those promises. In the meantime I'm thankful for temporary relief that God's gift of surgery could bring. It seems to me that this upcoming surgery could be one of his signs that the future resurrection producing our perfect bodies will indeed take place. I believe that Jesus' resurrection is Christians' insurance that we will live perfect forever."

Joe's comment echoes my thoughts, "Sounds great, if it's true; but, Bruce, why do you suppose your God—if he's the true God—let you live in strong pain for more than two decades?"

Joe asks good questions. I know that I've seen him somewhere in the past. I'll have to look in our high-school yearbook. Maybe he's there.

Bruce remarks, "I thought about that very question as I drove home. Ten years ago I asked God my angry 'why' that didn't seek information as much as it showed that I was mad at him. As God came close to me while I expressed my 'whys' sixty times, at the end he enabled me to submit peacefully to his will permitting pain in my body." *Amazing!*

"However, his peace also goes with my responsibility to seek God's relief, if there is any. After all, he created medical means to keep us healthy in order to serve him. His peace is not fatalistic."

Wow! Impressive! Can God really give me that kind of peace?

"Joe and Holly, I believe that God gave me insight into the reason he allowed pain in my body for those many years. One clue to that seeming mystery is that *not one* of the many doctors that I consulted in six states and Canada picked up on the fact that my back was the cause of my foot pain. They helped me decrease my pain and treated other conditions—both important jobs. Sure, I had some back pain, especially after each of three moves, but God used three chiropractors to help me recover each time.

"A second clue to that mystery is that immediately after my retirement, my local doctor sent me to a pain specialist who suspected my back as the culprit. That doctor demonstrated that there were two pinches in my lower back with an MRI and with three steroid injections that relieved my foot pain temporarily. I believe that God provided that doctor's insights at the right time. After his diagnosis was complete, he moved his practice to Florida!

"The new pain doctor injected me once higher with a shot that relieved my thigh pain for three and a half weeks. Then, that doctor referred me to the spine surgeon."

I ask, "How could your God be involved in the timing of those events?"

"Well, it seems to me that my Father allowed my pain to go on for twenty-three years, while all of those doctors missed the real cause, until I retired from preaching. God permitted pain in my life to keep me humbly dependent on him for words to speak and for daily strength in all of my preaching and teaching.

"I believe that this pain is like Paul's 'thorn in the flesh' that he describes in 2 Corinthians 12:1-10. First, God gave Paul a vision of Paradise, a spiritual realm where believers go after death. Second, his 'thorn in the flesh' was a messenger of Satan that God permitted in Paul's life to keep him humbly dependent on him rather than proud of his preaching and teaching abilities. Third, Paul pleaded three times with God to take away the 'thorn,' whatever physical problem it was."

Joe jumps in with a big smile, "Hey, Bruce, turn around while I look for a thorn stuck in *your* back!"

Joe's quite a character! I like him.

Undeterred, Bruce continues with a grin, "Yeah, Joe, pull it out if you find it.... Anyway, God turned down the Apostle Paul's requests by saying, 'My grace is sufficient for you, for my power is made perfect in weakness.' Then, Paul concluded, 'For when I am weak, then I am strong' in verse ten."

Joe blurts out, "Say *what?!*"

Bruce grins. "I won't repeat that joke, Joe. My point is that God used my pain to teach me that my strength was very weak and that I would not be able to be God's agent of lasting blessing in other people's lives apart from his power operating in and through me. God taught me through pain that I had to depend on him for all of the words to speak in the ministry through constant prayer. He's all-powerful, while I'm far from it. The way I see it, God allowed me to have pain most of the time that I spent behind the pulpit. Now that I'm no longer preaching and have learned his lessons permanently, perhaps he's going to give me some relief from my pain. Of course, I still need his power for writing.

"However, I'm convinced that some day I'll have a new, perfect body that will have no more pain in God's paradise—all because of God's unearned love! I *yearn* for Jesus' return."

I don't know if there will be such a future for me. I'm still young and in good health. There's plenty of time for me to decide.

* * *

There comes Joe's fancy sports car. He stops in front of my apartment building and with a "Joe-flourish" ushers me into his comfortable front seat. "How are you doing, Joe?"

"I'm fine, Holly. You're looking beautiful tonight in that purple blouse and slacks."

"Thanks. Where are we going tonight? You wouldn't tell me earlier when you asked me out."

"Well, I'll give you a choice between dancing in the Quad-Cities and dinner and a movie here."

"Let's go to the movie; I hear that it's a good one. Where do you want to eat?"

Joe was turning on the ignition as he replied, "Do you like Chinese?"

"I love Chinese."

"Chinese, it is."

After the waiter serves us, I ask Joe, "How do you feel about Bruce's ideas?"

"At this point I don't know how to feel. Bruce and I have gone through a lot together. We're really good friends, but I'm still leery of his God. How do you feel?"

"I tend to believe in a higher power, but whether that God is Bruce's and the priests' version, I'm not sure. The spiritual authority-figures in the past have alienated me with their abuse and cover-up. I'm also leery of trusting Bruce that he is right for fear that he's going to disappoint me the way the priests did."

"I understand completely. Authority figures in my life have disappointed me too, Holly. I'm also scared that Bruce will prove to be like the others." Joe suddenly leans over the corner of the table and kisses me. I return his kiss. *I didn't see that kiss coming, but it was great!*

CHAPTER 35

New bodies

The next month and a half leading to my surgery dragged very slowly for me, thus testing my patience. I failed that test at times.

However, I poured out my impatience in prayer. The amazing result was that on the day before surgery, God provided me with his gift of peace that enabled me to accept lumbar surgery as part of his plan for my life. That same day, Joe and I met as we entered the locker room. He asked me a question that appeared to have been coming on for some time, as we walked slowly through the swinging door to the pool, "Is it our fault that our bodies fail us, Bruce?"

My reply echoed in the concrete-block aquatic center, "Joe, many people have thought that each experience of suffering is the result of a single sin. However, the Bible shows us clearly that Job's so-called friends, who blamed Job for his suffering, were wrong in saying that each major sin produces suffering.

"However, it is true that the sinful rebellion of humanity has caused our pain, suffering, and death. Only in that sense can we say that humans are at fault for their suffering. I don't want to read God's mind. My nerve, muscle, and arthritis pain definitely came as a result of the sin of the whole human race, including mine. How I react to that pain is very important, whether with a mixture of anger and faith like Job, in self-righteous judgmentalism like Job's friends, in complete unbelief like many people today, or in worship of false gods. God has taught me that a combination of anger and faith focusing on him is by far the best choice, according to his Word, the Bible."

When we settled comfortably in the hot-tub, Holly emerged from the pool and settled into the steaming shallows, "Hi, guys." Joe then asked an ultimate question, "How is it possible that God will give perfect bodies to people who believe in him?"

"Joe, the Bible describes very clearly the resurrection of the body in 1 Corinthians 15. Paul begins that chapter describing the problem of the believers at Corinth, who believed in Jesus' resurrection but not in believers' resurrection. Greeks believed that all matter, including the stuff of our bodies, was totally evil. Therefore, they thought that at death our souls flit away to heaven, while our bodies stay permanently in the ground. You can see why they had trouble believing in the future resurrection of these same bodies."

Joe countered, "Yeah, I believe that I will stop existing and decay in the ground."

Holly pitched in, "I'm not sure what to believe. I don't think that I still believe in purgatory."

"I don't either, Holly, because I don't find that teaching in the Bible." I said and then countered the Greeks and Joe, "Well, inspired Paul said that because the Corinthians believed in Jesus' resurrection (which we have discussed), they should also believe in believers' resurrection."

Joe inquired, "How could he possibly show that Christians will rise from the dead permanently?"

"In 1 Corinthians 15 he first related the abundant evidence that Jesus definitely rose from the dead. He pointed to Jesus' many appearances to his followers over forty days from his resurrection until he went to heaven. Jesus even showed himself in his resurrection body to over 500 followers at the same time and ate broiled fish in the presence of his followers, thus showing that his risen body was physical.

"Then, Paul argued that because Jesus arose, his followers will also rise from death. He wrote that if Jesus did not rise from the grave, believers won't either. However, he then declared, 'But Christ has indeed been raised from the dead, the firstfruits of those who have fallen asleep....For as in Adam all die, so in Christ all will be made alive' (1 Corinthians 15:20,22). Jesus is the firstfruits, that is, the first of the resurrection harvest."

Joe sailed another question toward me, "At Sunday School they taught me that our souls just go off to heaven and stay there. They were wrong?"

"They may have been influenced by the Greeks without knowing it. No, Paul went on to write that the resurrection bodies that believers will inherit are these same bodies without any imperfections. In 1 Corinthians 15:24 and the following verses, Paul wrote that when Jesus will finish defeating his enemies, including death, at his coming, he will hand over the kingdom to the heavenly Father, "so that God may be all in all" (verse 28c).

"Then, Paul gave an amazing description of the human body raised from death by comparing our bodies to seeds sown in the ground when we die and then describing the differences between our present bodies and the future bodies. He writes in verses 42-44 that these bodies (like seeds) will be sown perishable but raised imperishable, sown in dishonor but raised in glory (God's brightness), sown in weakness but raised in power, and sown a natural body but raised a spiritual body, that is, completely controlled by the Spirit. Paul makes it clear that these bodies will be made new and improved without sin and its results, not completely different bodies."

"That teaching is really amazing!" Joe exclaimed.

"God's Word denies reincarnation that teaches our re-entry to this world immediately after death, the escapism believing that only our souls survive forever, and some people's idea that we merely sleep in the grave after death. Instead, when we die, God judges us by sending us to heaven or hell. Then, believers' souls stay in heaven until Jesus returns to re-manufacture this earth into a new earth and to re-unite our souls with our new resurrection bodies that will be new and improved like Jesus' body. Then, Jesus will judge all humans publicly."

"That belief is unbelievable!" Joe's skepticism said.

"It's believable if you trust in the all-powerful 3-in-1 Creator."

Holly changed the subject, "Bruce, how do you feel about your surgery in ten days?"

"I'm a little anxious, because I met a woman at the New Life Nursing Home who was paralyzed because a surgeon nicked the nerve leading to her right leg during back surgery. I believe that God sent me to her to impress on me the need for persistent prayer. Apparently, that kind of mistake is a rare result of surgery, but I will be asking people in all my churches to pray for my successful surgery."

Joe volunteered, "I hope that you have successful surgery without paralysis, Bruce."

Holly agreed, "I do too, Bruce."

"Thanks. You're good friends. I'm hoping and praying for at least some relief from my pain, which has been distracting me from God's retirement activities."

* * *

> But our citizenship is in heaven. And we await a Savior from there, the Lord Jesus Christ, who by the power that enables him to bring under his control, will transform our lowly bodies so that they will be like his glorious body.
>
> (Philippians 3:20,21)

* * *

Part Seven Questions:

1. How do you feel about the way the narrator handled his visit to Phil in jail? How could he have done it differently?
2. How effective is the narrator's answer about the miracles in Egypt, especially the opening of the Red Sea? What else could he have said?
3. How did the narrator's attempt to prepare Joe for his reading of the Law in Exodus lead to Joe's response that he always thought that he could lead a good enough life to earn God's approval, if there is a God? Summarize in your own words Paul's teaching in Ephesians 2:1-10, to which the narrator appeals to answer Joe's objection.
4. According to the narrator, how are Christian beliefs different from every other religion's beliefs? How does that difference make you feel? What point that the narrator has been making all along with Joe about the uniqueness of the Christian faith could have been made at this point as well?
5. One Bible teacher said that it's important to read every law and name in the Bible because God put them there. In the light of that advice, what do you think of the narrator's advice to Joe at the end of chapter seven? Is his advice a good approach to certain parts of the Bible? Why or why not?

PART 8

How many ways are there to God?

CHAPTER 36

A New Heart

On my first day back at the pool after my successful back surgery, Joe and I had just begun basking in the temporarily-restorative warmth of the hot-tub, as Holly finished her laps. A shapely, beautiful, brunette young woman in a horizontally-striped, green bikini entered the pool area for the first time while we were there and dove into the pool at the deep end near our vantage point.

After her lithe body sliced the water with only two answering ripples like a knife cutting soft butter, Joe commented in a whisper with a big grin, "Look at the beautiful scenery, Bruce!"

"Yep, God sure made a pretty world."

Joe straightened his neck, threw back his head, and asked, "Whatcha mean, preacher-man?"

"Joe, I used to lust after women in addition to my wife. I centered my attention on the women's bodies and relished in my selfish pleasure while watching them. But God brought to my attention Jesus' words in Matthew chapter five that lusting after women who aren't our wives is the same as committing adultery. Then Jesus enabled me to praise God with my mind for his amazing ability to create a beautiful woman while I watched her. My focus, which God enabled me to have, is now on him rather than on my selfish pleasure. Another result is that my Father through Jesus by the Spirit's power set me free from my self-centered lust in order to praise him instead."

Joe intoned with a nasal quality like Gomer Pyle, "Bruce, you're a piece of work!"

At that moment the other beautiful woman at the pool, Holly, lowered her sleek body into the tub and greeted us, "What's up, guys? Say, Joe, I was looking through my high school yearbooks and found your picture. You were a senior when I was a freshman."

Joe responded in typical fashion, "Really! Holly, I don't think that you ever were a fresh *man*!"

We chortled together at the mental picture that Joe had created.

However, his next question returned to my statement with a different twist, "Bruce, you keep talking about God doing things for you 'through Jesus by the Holy Spirit.' How can you be so sure that Jesus is the only one that does things for you? Don't other religions have some good points too?"

I looked back and forth from Joe to Holly, "Of course, other religions and the cults promote good morals, and there are some fine, upstanding folks in those groups and cults. However, I'm afraid that they have the wrong gods and that they fail to supply people with the power to live for God in a way that truly pleases him. It makes all of the difference in the world which God you believe in, because you don't want to serve one of the demons. In all of the belief systems and cults besides Christianity, people have to earn their gods' love with human strength and effort, a desire which comes from human thinking.

"I've experienced the truth that the true God of the Christian faith supplies believers with divine power to please him from the Father through Jesus' victory by the Holy Spirit, not our own paltry power.

"You have already read in John 14:6, Joe, Jesus' controversial but true statement about himself, 'I am the way and the truth and the life. No one comes to the Father except through me. If you really know me, you will know my Father as well. From now on, you do know him and have seen him.'

"Thomas had previously said to Jesus that the disciples didn't know where Jesus was going when he said that he was going away. That controversial statement was Jesus' response. That same doubting Thomas later came to believe that Jesus rose from the dead a week after Easter because of three reasons. First, his doubt changed to faith in Jesus because he was able to touch him. Second, he saw him alive. Third, he saw him eat broiled fish.

"Holly and Joe, other groups promote self-help rather than God's free gift of Jesus to rescue humans and of the Holy Spirit for the power to follow him."

Joe asked, "Bruce, if Jesus is God as he claimed, couldn't he rescue a black person with a different religion in Africa who has never heard about him? Wouldn't he be unjust not to save that person, who never had a chance?"

"Yeah, Bruce, I always wondered about that situation too."

I declared, "I never judge whether God has rescued anyone. Only he knows their hearts. Of course, nowadays anyone in the world can tune to a message about Jesus on a radio. If they choose not to listen, they are tuning God out of their lives. The reason is that Jesus was very clear in saying that a personal relationship with him is the only way for us to have full life that lasts forever with the 3-in-1 God.

"The teachers among God's people during Jesus' life called for the people to have a relationship with their interpretations of the Law and rather than an intimate relationship with God. But unconventional Jesus called us to a personal relationship with him that transforms our lives. He makes those changes within us through God the Father's gift of a new heart by the Spirit's power."

Joe's comical mood brought on the next question as he clutched his heart and fell backwards against the hot-tub's tiled wall, "What was God doin'? Was he givin' you a heart *transplant*?"

"Yep, he was replacin' my hard, passively-rebellious heart with a new, pliable heart that began to submit to his way of thinkin', feelin', and doin'....I already told you that he talked me into believing that he is real, Jesus is God, and the Bible is God's Word when I was sixteen.

"At the same time he also changed my life. I remember an event when I was about twelve and my younger brother, Steve, was eight. Our mother was so fed up with our rebellion against gardening that she made us *sit* in the garden, if we weren't going to *work* there, while *she* worked. '*So there!*'

"Well, just sitting there that summer morning near the line of osage-orange trees that bordered our mother's huge garden was downright boring. The result was that we got the bright idea to escape to freedom. When Mom turned her back, we made our guilty escape through the trees to play for the rest of the morning in our older brother's forty-foot-high, two-room treehouse deep in our eighteen-acre oak forest. In the afternoon we played in our over-stuffed, two-car garage that had a grand total of zero vehicles because of all the junk. There we played in our box-forts."

I stopped to make sure that Joe and Holly were still with me. Holly said with a steady stare, "Go on, Bruce. What happened next?"

I responded with a half-grin, "Well, about the time for our summer supper at sundown, we went to the side door in the breezeway of our ranch-style house for our evening meal, when we discovered that it was locked. Not only did we bang on all the doors in futility, but the house was totally dark in the waning light. We were locked out for the night!"

Joe replied, "What'd you two do?"

I lapsed into a base soap-opera announcer's voice, "Supper was in some frozen orange-extract boxes that we found in the garage freezer, and our fort became our bedroom for the night. The next morning we wandered, disheveled, into the sunlit, cluttered, dirty kitchen. Well, Mom amazingly greeted us as if nothing had happened, 'Here's your breakfast, boys!'

"Our church-going Mom never said anything about that incident. However, in our hard-hearted revenge we poured cement into her fertilizer early the next spring. All that following summer she complained, 'This ground is really hard!' as we snickered behind her back, while enjoying every minute!"

Holly and Joe doubled up with their faces near the bubbling water's surface and let out belly-laugh howls. Holly observed, "You guys were real rascals!"

"However, when God, my Father, through Jesus by the Spirit changed my rebel's passive-aggressive heart at sixteen years old, I was *much more* willing to help Mom in that organic garden. Even though we were doing the work the 'long way,' I suddenly had a desire to help her, not for the gardening's sake but for God's and her sake! God did it all!"

CHAPTER 37

No excuses

As usual, Joe brought us back to our topic, "Bruce, we started talking about the Africans who had no chance to hear about Jesus, if indeed God is real and Jesus is the only way to him. What do you say about their inability to get a new heart because they never had the chance to hear about him?"

"Yeah, Bruce, what about them?" echoed Holly.

"I don't judge them, but I just leave them in God's merciful hands. Not everything in life is clear. But it *is* clear that Jesus is the *only* way to the Father!" I slapped my right fist into my open left hand, while sending up an arrow-prayer to respond with God's words, "All I know is that Christians are called to spread the Word about him to others because of that fact....Of course, Romans 1:18-20 says that God has revealed his creative power through his creation's design and that, therefore, all people are without excuse for their unbelief about him, because his existence-evidence is all around us." I recovered, relieved, with arrow-thankfulness sent up to God that he gave me the words to speak.

Joe's characteristic, answering silence made me guess that his resistance was beginning to melt somewhat. However, he changed the subject again, "You've mentioned the movie *The Ten Commandments* that you say God used to change you. Do you like to watch movies?"

"I like to watch *good* ones! What about both of you?"

Holly and Joe both nodded. Joe said, "O yeah, I enjoy the old comedies like the ones Laurel and Hardy used to make as well as the Three Stooges and the Little Rascals."

"Well, I have several Laurel and Hardy movies." I replied. "My favorite is *Way Out West*. How about coming over to watch the colorized version in my surround-sound room?"

Joe dead-panned, "I'll hafta look at my busy calendar to see what I'm doin', but I thought you'd never ask!" and fell backward against the hot-tub wall in mock relief. Holly and I laughed at the hot-tub comedian.

CHAPTER 38

Comedy

The following Wednesday night Joe escorted Holly to our condo to watch Stan Laurel and Oliver Hardy's comedic genius at work. We emitted many belly-laughs at Ollie's pratfalls in a river's suddenly-deep hole as they both waded through it early *and* late in the film; at Ollie and Stan's attempts to give the deed of a gold mine to Mary Roberts, while falling for a ruse by the wife of the saloon owner when she impersonated Mary, a worker at the bar; at Stan's extreme laughter from the tickling inflicted by the saloon owner's wife in getting the deed away from him; and at Stan's attempt to climb to the second floor of the saloon by rope to retrieve the deed, while only succeeding to lift their donkey there.

When the film ended, I asked, "Well, what do you think, Joe and Holly?"

Holly responded, "I never watched Laurel and Hardy before, but I really enjoyed this film."

Joe said, "I must admit that I enjoyed it more this time in color."

I said, "Yeah, it's a little better. Of course, I remember black-and-white TV and movies."

"Boy, you're as old as the hills, Bruce!" Joe exclaimed in mock disbelief.

"Well, I'm not wet behind my ears like someone else I know! However, it seems to me that comedy is about human weakness, like Ollie's falling into the deep hole in the river the second time at the end of the film. That comedy scene's about human forgetfulness. We laugh because both of his falls surprise us, but we can also relate to his human weakness. In the end, comedies remind me of my weaknesses and sins. Therefore, after my laughing dies down, I confess my weaknesses and ask for God's forgiveness through Jesus."

Holly replied, "I never thought of it that way."

I testified, "In 1951 when I was nine years old, Dad brought home our first TV. I was totally bored with the farm and hated the work. The Cubs were on TV then. As a result, sports and TV became false gods in my life. I depended on them for escape from life on the farm into pleasure until the early 1980s in my first church as a pastor.

"In that church I preached a series on the biblical principles for leisure time. I came to I Corinthians 10:30, where God led Paul to write that we are to do everything to honor God. I asked myself whether or not I was honoring God as I watched TV and sports and answered 'no.' I know that it was God working in my life through his Word. My only two choices in the light of that verse were either to eliminate TV and sports completely from my life or to find some way to honor God with them. Then, I discovered that I could praise God for his amazing creative power in making the human body as I watched sports.

"Thus, I began to look for the TV programs and movies with which I could honor him in some way. For example, I began to watch crime dramas while praising God for his divine quality of justice in punishing sin and his creation of human ingenuity, reasoning, and science in the solving of those crimes."

Joe jumped in, "Bruce, if God does exist, he apparently changed your approach to TV and sports in a way similar to his overcoming your lust for women."

Holly interrupted with a grin, "Say *what*?!"

Joe went along with the joke, "*What*?! Bruce and I were talking the other day before you came to the hot-tub about his belief that God changed him from lusting after women to praising God for his creation when he saw them." Then, he turned to me, "But wasn't it just human willpower, Bruce?"

"Joe, it was not by my effort but solely by God's great grace. I couldn't have done it on my own. God's power to change us by his grace is the difference between Christianity, on the *one hand*, and the other belief systems, on the *other hand*."

Joe held out both of his hands with his palms up and asked with a broad smirk, "Which one are ya usin'?"

I returned his smile, raised my index fingers toward the ceiling, and observed, "It was *Jesus' hands* as the only ones that get us goin' to the Father and changin' our lives permanently! We can't do a spiritual or physical heart transplant on ourselves, can we?"

CHAPTER 39

Real Prayer

After Joe, Holly, and I shared more semi-serious playfulness, I asked Joe seriously, "Joe, how's the job-hunting going?"

"I'm afraid that the economy's descent into the black hole of recession has swallowed many available jobs."

My seriousness deepened into an emotional recession in empathy for Joe's struggle as I asked, leaning forward, "Are you looking just around here or everywhere?"

"I'm putting my emphasis on the Quad-Cities for now, but I may have to look elsewhere soon."

"Joe, I've found in the past, when I've been looking for jobs, that it takes a lot of effort with frequent contacts to keep my resume on the top of the pile. And, of course, it takes a lot of prayer."

He said, "I wish I could be...sure that there's...a God that I can pray to."

"I think that you'll get there, Joe. Praying is just talking through your friend, Jesus, to your perfect heavenly Father, who makes you perfect in his sight because of Jesus' flawlessness—that's all."

Holly asked, "The priests always prayed for us. How does prayer work, Bruce?"

I charged into that familiar subject like a bull in a bakery spreading the sugar around, "Well, it's important to understand God's roles. First, our Father made everything and everyone through Jesus by the power of the Holy Spirit with the Father spotlighted in creation. Second, the Father sent the second Person of God by way of a perfect birth with the power of the Spirit as the God-baby, Jesus, who was spotlighted for our rescue by dying on the cross. Third, the Father sent the Holy Spirit through his Son. The Spirit gets the spotlight as he creates new hearts in true believers and makes us more and more like him. The work of that one God is to restore Christians to be the way he created us—remember?—originally in Genesis chapter one."

Joe focused on the topic as usual, "How does that relationship affect our prayers, if we believe in that God?"

I pointed my right index finger upward, "Well, the Holy Spirit enables believers to talk, by his power, to the Father through Jesus as the only way to him. We pray to the one true God in that way!"

Joe's skepticism replied, "Well, I'm not ready, since it seems to me that praying is just like blowing into a balloon with a lot of empty air that just pops after awhile."

Holly said, "I'm not so sure God answers my prayers anymore, Bruce."

"Joe and Holly, you're invited to our Bible-discussion group at George Murphy's home Sunday night, but it's entirely up to you."

Holly and Joe replied, almost in unison, "I'll think about it."

CHAPTER 40

An uncomfortable trial

The county courtroom was packed for Phil's trial, even though his court-appointed lawyer had succeeded in getting a change of venue to the Poweshiek County Court House, Iowa District 8, in Montezuma, Iowa, because of local gossip and publicity.

I marched down the hallway in the antique 1857 courthouse and passed the Mad Court on my left. I wondered vacantly how "mad" it was and guessed that it might be the court where a judge tried traffic tickets.

Ahead of me was the main courtroom, where I wedged my body into the bench next to Joe, who had saved me a space. Holly and he had made the journey together. I arrived there just in time to hear the bailiff state in a weary monotone, as if he would rather be anywhere but there, "All rise, the Iowa District Court in and for Poweshiek County is now open. The Honorable Charles Bloom presiding."

Joe had filled me in on the two-week trial until the lawyers' closing arguments today. Inspite of Phil's protests of innocence, the prosecuting attorney had proceeded with the trial. A neighbor had been called to testify that she saw Phil talking with the alleged victim in the street and leading him into his house like a 'cow into the slaughter house.' Judge Bloom struck that description from the record, but it was likely still seared into the jury's memories. The accusing boy had pointed Phil out with a riveting, x-rated description of Phil's "crime" with no cross-examination by Phil's court-appointed lawyer.

On the day that I visited the trial in the Montezuma courthouse, Phil's lawyer called him to testify in an unusual move. He again emphatically described the fateful day's events and the boy's "made-up" tale about Phil's guilt. Of course, he at the same time protested that he was "not guilty." However, Joe whispered, almost inaudibly, to me that his father certainly wasn't innocent of his earlier, hidden sins.

Then, during the closing arguments, the prosecuting attorney, a middle-aged, thin man with a close-cropped goatee, launched into his speech describing the "facts" and "gossip" of the case.

By contrast, the defense attorney, a tall, soft-spoken man, spoke briefly about this upstanding citizen, who was falsely accused by an angry juvenile, and pointed out to the jury that there was no physical evidence that a crime had been committed. By the end of the lawyers' tirades, a certain part of my anatomy was beginning to suffer, just the way some people's anatomies do on hard church pews at the end of a 30-minute sermon. I was beginning to wonder if I might get Montezuma's revenge and at the same time hoped that *Phil* wouldn't experience it!

Finally, Judge Bloom informed jury members of their duties and dispatched them to "deliberate dispassionately." As Holly, Joe, and I arose to stretch our bodies in the hallway next to the Mad Court, Joe declared, "I hope that my father gets a 'not guilty' verdict."

I asked, "How's the job search going, Joe?"

His voice dropped an octave with a mysterious quality, "I have a few…leads. However, a local employer…called me back for another interview, but I'm trying not to get too excited."

"That's good news, Joe!" Holly exclaimed.

We low-fived, while I said in almost a whisper, "You know, Joe, that I have been praying for you and your family daily all of this time that I've known you."

"Time will tell whether or not your prayers will help," said our anxious, half-grinning friend. The jury deliberated another three hours that sunny, early-June, 2009, day without a decision.

* * *

> Jesus answered, "I am the way and the truth and the life. No one comes to the Father except through me….Believe me when I say that I am in the Father and the Father is in me; or at least believe on the evidence of the works themselves."
>
> (John 14:6,11)

Part Eight Questions:

1. What do you think about the narrator's explanation of the human body's imperfection? Explain. What was Joe's response to the narrator's explanation?
2. What do you think of the narrator's explanation of the significance of his future back surgery? How did Joe react?
3. How do you react to the narrator's explanation of the pain that he experienced for more than two decades and to God's possible relief from that pain?
4. How does the narrator describe the peace and the responsibility that he experienced in connection with his pain? How does that combination relate to any suffering or struggle that you might go through?
5. How is the narrator's pain compared to Paul's 'thorn in the flesh'? What joke does Joe make about that comparison? What 'thorns in the flesh' do you see Christians enduring today? How can we endure them?
6. How does the narrator's quote of 2 Corinthians 12:8-10 cause Joe to make another joke? How does the narrator explain the spiritual meaning of his pain? How satisfactory to you is that explanation? What other passages from the Bible might you have referred to?

PART 9

What is Jesus going to do in the future?

CHAPTER 41

Justice

The following Wednesday was the next time I saw Joe. While I was putting my swimsuit on, in he slouched with his head down like a thief in the late afternoon trying to avoid small-town stares. I greeted him and asked for his description of the rest of the trial.

"Hi, Bruce. I've never seen anything like that trial. The jury returned to the courtroom at mid-afternoon on Monday. They might as well have been in the 'Mad' Court down the hall. The foreperson handed a slip of paper to the judge as I shook in my boots. He handed the paper back to the foreperson with a non-committal look on his face and asked for the jury's verdict. The word 'guilty' resounded throughout the courtroom. Phil and his lawyer gasped audibly. They then faced the judge for his sentence.

"Judge Bloom with his deep, booming voice pronounced his sentence, 'I am now ready to sentence you, Mr. Smith. Under Iowa law I cannot vacate the jury's guilty verdict. However, I do not understand that decision. The evidence pointed to a 'he-said-he-said' situation and failed to prove beyond a reasonable doubt your guilt.

"'On the other hand, I will, under Iowa law, suspend your sentence, put you on probation for two years, and expunge your verdict and sentence from the records if you keep your record clean....So ordered!'

"Judge Bloom banged his gavel so hard with echoing thunder that the gavel's head flew off and landed in front of the table of the prosecuting attorney."

I grinned, "Well, I'm thankful that Phil wasn't taken immediately to death-row, the way some of our town's gossip had it!"

CHAPTER 42

A future event

Bruce's Bible-discussion group made up of his church's members meets at George Murphy's large, sprawling, three-story house in early September after their evening church. They just finish the opening prayer, which we see through the living room window as we approach the front door, when the doorbell's loud clang announces our entrance. Bruce introduces Joe and me to the group, which is largely made up of small-town working and business people. George, a successful businessman in his late-40s, leads the discussion about Matthew 24. He explains that in that chapter Jesus combined his prophecy about the destruction of Jerusalem forty years later in A.D. 70 with the events of his Second Coming, which is yet in our future.

Joe and I sit quietly throughout the discussion until George asks a thought-provoking question, "How can you believe in Jesus' Second Coming? After all, it's been almost 2,000 years since Jesus promised that event."

Joe chimes in with a frown, "Yeah, that's a long time to wait."

Joe sure is a skeptic, but he's very likeable.

Fred, a 58-year-old car salesman, answers with a rhetorical question, "Wasn't it the Apostle Peter who wrote about the scoffers questioning the long wait? He replied to them and us that a day is like a thousand years and a thousand years is like a day with the Lord. God shows his amazing patience in order to give people time to change their thinking and actions to follow him."

Sally, a young full-time mom and homemaker who fumbles around in her Bible, replies, "That's right. I was reading the other day in Second Peter chapter three about Peter's response to doubters. Here it is! It's in verses nine and ten,

'The Lord is not slow in keeping his promise, as some understand slowness. He is patient with you, not wanting anyone to perish, but everyone to come to repentance. But the day of the Lord will come like a thief. The heavens will disappear with a roar; the elements will be destroyed by fire, and the earth and everything in it will be laid bare. So since everything in it will be destroyed in this way, what kind of people ought you to be? You ought to live holy and godly lives as you look forward to the day of God and speed his coming.'"

Joe exclaims, "That's really scary! The whole universe will be burned up!?"

Will I be ready for that frightening event?

Bruce replies, "Of course, First Thessalonians 4 says that those who have accepted the God-man Jesus as the only way to God the Father will rise into the atmosphere against the law of gravity to meet Jesus and all other believers in the air. Jesus will come back with the souls of all true believers, who will then arrive from heaven to be reunited with their new bodies."

I don't know if I can believe what Bruce says, but it all seems to come from the Bible.

That passage is found in verses fourteen through eighteen:

'We believe that Jesus died and rose again and so we believe that God will bring with Jesus those who have fallen asleep [or "died"] in him. According to the Lord's own word, we tell you that we who are still alive, who are left till the coming of the Lord, will certainly not precede those who have fallen asleep. For the Lord himself will come down from heaven, with a loud command, with the voice of the archangel and with the trumpet call of God, and the dead in Christ will rise first. After that, we who are still alive and are left will be caught up together with them in the clouds to meet the Lord in the air. And so we will be with the Lord forever. Therefore encourage each other with these words.'"

Bruce follows his reading with a question, "What events will happen when Jesus returns?"

Sally says, while leaning forward, "I've been reading the *Left Behind* series, books which say that the rapture about which your passage talks is an invisible coming of Jesus. Those books say that a seven-year tribulation will take place, during which the antichrist will reign supreme. They also say that believers will be whisked off to heaven. Then, a thousand-year period will take place in which the people will worship God in the re-built temple again in Jerusalem. When that millenium is finished, Christ will come visibly, following a brief skirmish with Satan and his demons, to bring about the White-Throne Judgment and start the new creation."

Bruce ventures with a steady voice, "That's one theory. I never heard of the future coming of Christ in the church of my youth."

I don't ever remember hearing about Christ's Second Coming in the Catholic church either. Of course, I wasn't listening very well either.

"However, the events that you describe (called pre-millenialism) were going to happen just that way, according to the church where we attended when I became a Christian and according to the cult that we attended for 1½ years. By contrast, when I attended Calvin College, where my teachers taught that the period of a thousand years is the present time (called a-millenialism) that will end when Christ comes visibly to make all believers perfect."

Bruce has certainly had a lot of experiences in many different churches.

"After I learned all of those ideas, I didn't think that it made much difference which one of those interpretations was correct, because we'll all find out which interpretation is correct when all will be fulfilled. One of our sons says that he's a pan-millenialist; it'll all pan out!"

That joke's a good one. After all, what real difference does it make?

All of us had a hearty chuckle at our son's joke.

"However, when I was in seminary, we studied the Book of Revelation. I compared that book to the five major theories and other minor ones about the events of Jesus' Second Coming and concluded that the Book of Revelation is a very symbolic book like many other writings of that time. Also, it became clear that the number 'thousand' referring to the thousand years is symbolic. I believe that it describes the complete time between Jesus' first and second arrivals, not a future time. (After all, the only place in the *whole* Bible that refers to a future thousand years is Revelation 20. In addition to that understanding, Revelation is a very symbolic book with symbolic numbers. I believe that it's pretty shaky Bible interpretation to base a whole set of events on one short, hard-to-understand passage.)

"However, there are much more important ideas in the Bible that are a matter of life and death and about which we need to agree. Therefore, I think that it's very important for Christians to agree to disagree on this one. After all, we'll all some day find out which interpretation is correct! We'll discover, for example, whether the thousand years is happening now or whether it is a literal, future time. However, we won't want to say to one another at Jesus' coming, 'I told you so', will we?

"The whole point is that Jesus will come to judge everyone. I'm convinced that we need to be ready for him clothed with *his* perfection through faith in him. Otherwise, we will lose out on the new creation described symbolically in the last three chapters."

Am I ready for Jesus' coming? I'm afraid that I'm not.

George ended the ensuing silence with a quick question, "What difference does the hope of Jesus' Second Coming make in our lives?"

Bruce echoes George, "What does Peter mean by our need to live 'holy and godly lives' and Paul, by giving each other 'mutual encouragement,' that they call us to do because of the teaching about Jesus' Second Coming?"

Only the Catholic saints lead such lives, I always thought. However, Bruce says that all true believers in Jesus are saints. I'm confused.

Larry, a 20-something fifth-grade teacher, replies with his eyes glued on the brown carpeting, "It doesn't mean anything if we don't believe it or never think about it, does it?" Many group members nod and lapse into subdued silence.

George picks up on the group's mysterious, melancholy mood by asking, "What is it about this doctrine that makes us avoid meditating on it?"

Joe pipes up, "I have trouble believing in Jesus' resurrection, much less that he is coming again. Why do you folks believe that Jesus rose from the dead and is coming again?"

Yeah, why? Joe asks good questions. At least, you always know what Joe's thinking.

Responding to Joe's question, George says with his arms out and palms up, "On the one hand, Jesus promised that he would come again. On the other, God has changed my life from alcoholism. Jesus, my living Savior, made me into a 12-step abstainer with his gift of the new birth. That enormous blessing of regeneration in my life shows me that Jesus' free gift of resurrection power has already taken place in my life but that he will perfect me some day.

"That experience is the reason that I believe in Jesus' resurrection on Easter and have hope for Christ's advent, as he promised. Of course, I'm God's constant project in which he helps me, through prayer, to overcome my many daily temptations. Those enticements make me want to escape life's tribulations into alcohol. But some day believers will be free of all their struggles, as the Bible says in Revelation 21:4—

'no more death or mourning or crying or pain'—I sure look forward to our future in the new creation!" All of the group members except Joe and me nod with quiet intensity.

Impressive! Maybe Jesus did come back to life and is coming again, the way the Catholic church taught, especially on Easter Sunday.

After a pause, Sally echoes George's hope, "I think godly and holy living means denying self, seeking God's help to overcome our selfishness, and focusing our life on God—all actions to which Jesus called us. I find that constant prayer is the key to that kind of living." The group members nodded.

I feel guilty about my angry feelings toward the church, but they failed the people. Shouldn't I be angry at the priests who molested those boys and the ones who covered those sins up? How can I believe anything that they taught me?

Bruce asks the group, "Then, how can we encourage each other to be more godly and holy?"

Fred responds with a grin, "We're doing it here by sharing and discussing the Bible. We also do it as we pray for each other." Most of the group nod vigorously.

At the end of our prayer time, we have refreshments, as the group members get better acquainted with Joe and me.

I really like these people. I wish I could believe what they believe.

We then say good-night and leave. Bruce's exit is close behind us.

CHAPTER 43

A sad announcement

I caught up with Joe and Holly on the sidewalk in front of the two-story house next to George's house. He turned to ask me a quiet question, "Can you keep a secret, Bruce and Holly?"

Holly and I nodded quickly as I said, "You know I can!"

"I went to my urologist today, and he's going to run some blood tests on me. He did what the nurses called a 'cysto' on me and suspects that I have prostate cancer," Joe intoned with a shoe-top gaze. He continued with some advice, "Bruce, don't let a doctor do one of those tests on you if you can prevent it. That test is embarrassing!"

"O, no, Joe!...That can't be right!...He might be wrong!...You're too young!" I blurted out rapidly but quietly (while ignoring Joe's last comment). I suddenly had thoughts about my experiences with the fallibility of the medical profession and billows of denial swirling around in my mind like a dreaded, disastrous, bottomless whirlpool.

"I have many of the symptoms of prostate cancer, but blood tests and perhaps a biopsy will tell the tale."

Holly blurted out, "You're definitely too young for prostate cancer!"

"The urologist said the same thing, but we will see what happens," Joe replied.

I promised, "I'll pray daily for your condition, Joe!"

"Thank you," Joe accepted my promise and added a question, "Bruce, do you *really* believe that Jesus is coming back to this earth?"

"Yes, I believe that he's coming back as firmly as I believe that we are standing here in front of the house of George's neighbor on Maple Street—all because Jesus, the risen God-man, promised it!"

Joe's serious silence showed me that he continued to struggle against believing in Jesus as the only way to God the Father by the Holy

Spirit and in the Bible as God's inspired Word. As the three of us parted with a hearty handshake and a friendly hug, I prayed secretly and sincerely for Joe's health as I returned to the house, where the group was just leaving.

CHAPTER 44

God's golf course

Jovial Joe frowns and fidgets as he picks me up to go golfing with Bruce.
I enjoy invading the fairways and greens of the Mississippi River Golf Club with Joe and Bruce one last time in late September before the cold of Iowa's winter envelopes it. At the second tee Joe pauses before his drive to pose a question, "What do you think happens to us when we die, Bruce?" as he tees up his golf ball. *Why would he ask such a question? Cancer and death must be on his mind. I don't know what will happen to me when I die.*

While we walk to our balls in the fairway (for Joe and me) and in the deep rough (as usual, for Bruce), Bruce raises his voice, "I believe that when we die and as our bodies are lowered into the grave, our souls go before God for his judgment of 'guilty' or 'not guilty.' He certainly has every right to judge us as our Creator with his perfect justice.

"The Word of God says in Hebrews 9:27, 28, 'Just as people are destined to die once and after that to face judgment, so Christ was sacrificed once to take away the sins of many; and he will appear a second time, not to bear sin, but to bring salvation to those who are waiting for him.'" *I haven't been a really bad person, but am I ready to face God in death?*

Joe's eyebrows pinch together as his second shot flies into a greenside sandtrap, while my shot clunks over the green up against the ball-cleaner pole. Bruce's shot sails into the woods to the right of the green. Following our bogies and Bruce's triple bogie as we walk to the next tee, Joe comments with a puzzled expression, "But you have said that we are all guilty."

"Yes, the Bible says that we are guilty because we are all imperfect people. *(Well, I'm certainly imperfect and, apparently, guilty before God.)* However, the Bible says that Jesus came to live a perfect, not-guilty life and to die as our flawless, innocent substitute. The result is that all who trust in his perfection enter God's presence as not-guilty believers when they die. Another result is that the Father, our divine Judge, now declares us 'not guilty.' Also, God will pronounce 'not guilty' all who trust in Jesus both when we die and again at the public judgment when Jesus returns, when not only our guilt but also our sins will be gone."

I interject, "Bruce, that teaching is amazing. How can God declare me 'not guilty,' even though I *am* guilty, a teaching that I heard a lot when I was a child?"

Bruce proceeds, "Holly, do you see how different God the Father is from our earthly fathers? He is our divine Judge, but he himself provided the solution for our guilt through Jesus' death. I believe that when believers die, our perfected souls, free from all imperfections, will enter into heaven in God's presence to await Jesus' Second Coming. It will be an amazing time when our souls will be united with our newly-resurrected bodies—these same bodies renewed. We will then enter the perfect, new universe that Jesus will make out of this old one, where there will be no cancer, other diseases, pain, or death!"

Joe intones, "It all seems so unbelievable."

"Joe and Holly, it seems to me that no one, even in his wildest dreams, could've conjured up a story about a God-man living a perfect life, dying a criminal's death as our substitute, rising from the dead, and coming again in the future. God—not humans—must've inspired the Bible's description of those events. The source couldn't have been human."

Bruce makes a lot of sense.

After a long, silent pause, Bruce peers at Joe and inquires softly, "How'd your tests turn out?"

Joe bows his head toward the ground after he swings mightily at the elusive little sphere, "Not so hot. My PSA count seems to indicate cancer, but I have a biopsy scheduled for next Thursday."

I retort rebelliously as my swing chunked the ball, which moved only a few frustrating feet, causing me to hit the ball again from the tee (an action describing golf-duffers' practice of taking a "mulligan" once in a round without counting the extra shot), "That's not good news. I hope that your health gets better."

Bruce says, "I know that God will answer my prayers for you. However, I don't know what his answer will be."

"Thanks, Holly and Bruce. You're good friends."

Yeah, we have become good friends, haven't we.

Our solemn round of golf and our trip to Joe's place end with mutual tears in front of the apartment house to which he had recently moved.

CHAPTER 45

Sheep or goats?

Bruce's Bible-discussion group meets in October, 2009, during the World Series, again without the Chicago Cubs. Joe and I arrive fifteen minutes early at Larry's house on the west side of town just a block from our church. After Larry, the humorous leader and host that evening, opens our get-together with prayer, we voluntarily take turns reading Matthew chapter 25. We briefly discuss the parables of the ten virgins and the bags of gold that point out the need to be constantly ready for Jesus' Second Coming. Next, Larry briefly explains Jesus' description of himself as the Ruler-Judge of the sheep on his right side (a favorable place) and the goats on his left side (an unfavorable place from which they will banished) at the Final Judgment. *Am I a goat or a sheep?*

Larry asks with a grin, after our reading about that event, "How do we know whether we are sheep or goats? Is it because we say either 'baa' or 'maa'? Is it because we will eat anything or only certain things?"

George observes, by reading verse 34, that the sheep are the "blessed" of the Ruler's Father and continues with a smile, "I don't believe that we are going to be judged on the basis of the kind of sounds that we make or the food that we eat."

Larry asks, "Then, the sheep aren't just those who do good things for other people?"

Sally says with an expressionless face, "No, we're all born like independent 'goats' until our Father blesses us with a sheep-like submissive nature because of Jesus' life, death, and resurrection. I see that goat-nature in each of our little children. Not one of them was born completely innocent!

"However, when God saves us, we can then begin to love him." *Lord, save me so that I will begin to love you and stop hating others.* "At the Second Coming, Jesus will usher all the goats-transformed-into-sheep into his kingdom. That future event makes me want to share Bible stories and my beliefs with my three mischievous children so that God will change them at a young age."

Larry observes with a chuckle and a comedic gleem in his eyes, "Some people are just 'old goats,' present company excluded, of course." He continues with a sober face, "However, I see in my life both a sheep's submissiveness and a goat's tendency to rebel. You know, there's a real temptation in life to tell lies to protect ourselves and gossip that will hurt others, to mention a couple ways we tend to rebel. However, I think that all Christians have that struggle between those two natures. We need to pray more." Again, the group grins and nods almost unanimously.

Fred sums up as he leans forward, "It's really sad that the goats will 'go away to eternal punishment,' as verse forty-six says." We all nodded solemnly.

I hope that I will be kept from that punishment.

Larry confides, "That future event will be no joke. The sad thing is that it will be the fault of those 'goats,' because they rebelliously refused to become submissive sheep and instead remained independent of God. Jesus has every right to judge them 'guilty' and to punish them eternally in hell, because they brought that judgment on themselves."

After the Bible discussion, Bruce catches up with us just before we get into Joe's car on the street. He asks, "Did you find out...how the biopsy...turned out?"

Joe answers, "I just found out after I got home from the pool. It *is* prostate cancer, but my cancer doctor doesn't think that it has spread."

My spirit sinks, "That's...bad and...good news, Joe. How are *you* doing?"

"I'm deeply depressed, because the thought of dying is scary!" Joe responds without making eye-contact with either of us.

Bruce observes, "It's scary for most people. That's why I believe that it's important for all of us to make sure that we are ready to meet our Maker!"

How can I be ready to meet God?

* * *

Then Jesus said to his disciples, "All who want to be my disciples must deny themselves and take up their cross and follow me....For the Son of Man is going to come in his Father's glory with the angels, and then he will reward everyone according to what they have done."

(Matthew 16:24,27)

Part Nine Questions:

1. How do you react to the narrator's true testimonies to God's work in changing him? What changes has God brought about in your life to which you could testify with unbelievers and believers alike? Why should we testify to God's work in our lives?
2. How effective is the narrator's explanation of what he feels about people dying without hearing about Jesus, if he is the only way to God? What else could he have said? How should we react to Jesus' claim that he is the only way to the Father? How do we react? Why?
3. What do you think about the narrator's explanation of the spiritual meaning of comedies? Why do you suppose the writer included the narrator's and Joe's watching the Laurel and Hardy movie? What do you think about such entertainment? How can entertainment like sports, movies, and TV become Christian for believers?
4. What is the narrator's response to Joe's objection that human changes are only human willpower? How did you respond to the banter of the narrator and Joe about their hands and Jesus' hands? What point do you think the writer is making with that conversation?
5. How do you think the reading of this chapter and book will affect you prayer life? How do you react to Joe's skepticism about prayer? How did that skepticism begin to waver at the end of the chapter?
6. On what verdict do you think the jury and the judge will decide in Phil's trial? Why? What purpose do you think the author had in describing Phil's trial in his book? Why?
Why or why not? What prayers does Jesus answer? How can we be always joyful, prayerful, and thankful, the way the First Thessalonians passage says? How can every activity, speech, and thought be a prayer to God? How much do we pray to God as the one only true Triune God? How can we pray to the Trinity?

PART 10

Does God punish humans?

CHAPTER 46

Robots and humans

The following Tuesday I meet Bruce as we enter the exercise facility to conquer the watery depths again. He breaks the silence quickly with his usual cheery greeting, "Hi, Joe. How're ya doing?"

"Not so good, Bruce. They want to take out my prostate. I'm scheduled for surgery two weeks from tomorrow in Iowa City, and get this. A robot's gonna operate on me!"

Bruce lurches backward from my words while struggling to maintain his balance, as if a large lead-weight had hit him. Recovering after a pause, he responds with a slight grin, "Maybe they'll get all of it, Joe."

"At least, they do it with only a tiny invasion of my body and with shorter recovery time than other procedures. However, I don't like robots cutting into me, even if they *do* leave only tiny puncture holes."

We imitate robots as we put on our faded, chlorine-ridden swimsuits and then head for our pre-swim shower with Bruce's comment, "Joe, I'll pray through Jesus that the surgery will take care of your problem. I'll also leave you in the capable hands of God, the divine Surgeon."

As we let the spitting showers cleanse our bodies for our swim, I share with Bruce what has been on my mind since our last Bible discussion, "Bruce, how do you know that there is a hell. I've always thought that if there's a God, he would let everyone into his heaven, because I heard when I was a kid that he's a God of love."

He confides with his index fingers pointed up, "I believe in the God revealed in the Bible, who is the only true God of love. That idea is the only belief that I also remember from the church of *my* youth.

"However, the God of the Bible is also a God of justice who cannot let imperfect people into his perfect heaven. Unlike a mythical, lenient Santa, he really has to punish all people's lifelong rebellion against him.

Jesus said, 'Be perfect as your heavenly Father is perfect.' We can't be perfect on our own, because only one sin-stain during our whole life makes us imperfect. Therefore, the saying that 'nobody's perfect' is very true." *Yeah, I'm far from perfect.* "That situation makes all of us worthy of separation from God forever.

"Instead, we need the perfect Rescuer, Jesus, as the God-man to die in our place in order to give us escape from hell and entrance into heaven when we die." *However, how can I accept Jesus' death in my place when God—if he does exist—has allowed so many tragedies in my life, which may also be my death.* "Humans in all of the other religions and in the cults have imagined that we can do good things to escape hell and go to heaven. By contrast, biblical faith says rightly that only God through Jesus can rescue us from hell."

I dive (and Bruce eases) our good-sized bodies into the pool as the women's water-exercise class concludes. Ten minutes later, beautiful Holly appears on the watery scene.

Thirty minutes later Bruce and I gladly immerse ourselves in the soothing heat of the hot-tub, as I say with a silly grin, "Bruce, if there's a heaven, do ya think that there are goin' to be hot-tubs there?"

With a smirk, Bruce echoes his wife's answer to their son Keith many years in the past, when he had asked about toys in heaven, "If hot-tubs will make us happy, there will be hot-tubs. But I'm sure that there are going to be much better things for us there."

I reply with the bubbling water right up to my gaping mouth, "I can't imagine that there's goin' to be anything better! Ah!!"

At that moment Holly lowers herself into the hot-tub, "Hi, guys! How are ya?"

I reply with my usual, "Fine, Holly!" *I wish I were fine!*

Holly shoots back, "Don't give me that answer, Joe! Tell me how you really are."

I admit, "I'm OK except that robots are set to operate on me in a couple weeks to take out my prostate."

Holly sighed, "That's more like it, Joe."

Bruce asks, "Joe, where are you reading in the Bible now?"

"I'm reading the Book of Job. Bruce, Job experienced a lot of heartaches, anger, and doubts. Yet he still believed in God! Amazing! Why does God—if there really is a God—let people suffer so much? I know that the book makes Satan the direct cause of Job's suffering, but why did God allow Satan to cause those terrible tragedies?"

Bruce responds, "It's my experience and belief that when believers suffer, God strengthens their faith. That change is what happened in my life during Keith's sickness and death. My prayers changed from 'thee' and 'thou' to 'you' as God came closer to me during that traumatic time. In addition, I already told you that with Keith's death, God conquered my rebellious will that was running away in teaching from God's call to the ministry in order for me to return to school to be a pastor. He is my perfect Father, who disciplines me by lovingly allowing hard experiences in order to make me more submissive to his will and love him more.

"In everyday family life, it's not good for parents to spoil a child by failing to set limits. There must be discipline too—that is, calls to children's responsibility and clear consequences for their actions. Similarly, you read that Job is described at the beginning of that book as 'blameless and upright.' In other words, he had a committed, genuine faith in God. But he was far from perfect, just like all believers! The result was that he had to learn to submit to God's plan for his life, no matter what tragedies God allowed for his good, instead of being angry when that plan wasn't the same as his plan. (I sinned the same repressed, self-centered sin of bitterness for the first two-thirds of my life.) God used his loving discipline to enable Job to repent at the end of the book for questioning the Creator-God of the universe."

"Ah, Bruce, you spoiled the book for me by givin' away the endin'!" hot-tub comic Joe said with a wink and a smile. *I wonder if I will end up a believer in the God of the Bible like Job inspite of my struggles.*

"Ah, Joe, I didn't tell ya the very endin' of the Book of Job. After all, I told you that much 'cause you asked!"

* * *

The following Saturday evening I pick up Holly, and we head toward Davenport to have dinner and dancing at the Westside Nightclub. As we eat, Holly shares her thoughts, "Joe, I've enjoyed our times together."

"Here's where…you…b-b-b-reak up…with me?!"

"No, Silly Joe, I'm not splitting us up."

"Whew, that's a relief! I really enjoy your company too. If we had only met each other and dated in high school, our lives might have been very different."

"Yeah, that thought has crossed my mind too."

"Well, the band's beginning to play a fast tune. Why don't we dance?"

"Good idea." *This woman's really getting to me! How would Jean feel about my dating Holly exclusively, I wonder. Well, she's not here to object.*

We dance the night away to both fast and slow, clingy tunes. At the end of the last song, Holly reaches up and gives me a full kiss on my mouth. We smooch a few more times as we float around the dance floor.

On our way back to town, I ask Holly with a sly wink, "Holly, do you want to spend the night with me?"

"No, Joe. One belief that I picked up in my youth is that we shouldn't sleep together before marriage."

Wow, she does have standards to live by!

"Well then, let's get married."

Holly laughs her full soprano laugh and responds, "We don't know each other well enough yet, Joe. I believe that it takes full commitment to one another, not just emotions, to marry someone."

CHAPTER 47

An amazing rescue

The next Monday in the hot-tub, I ask Bruce a query that had festered in my mind since his explanation of God's rescue, "Why doesn't God—if he does exist—send everyone to heaven through Jesus' dying and rising again? That way God wouldn't need to condemn anyone to hell—if there is such a place."

Holly echoes me, "Yeah, Bruce. That's a good question, Joe."

"I don't know, because the Bible doesn't say. He certainly has more than enough power to rescue everyone. However, I do know that there must be a very good, unrevealed reason. I also know that the human race's rebellion makes it their own fault, not at all God's fault, that he has to punish them eternally in hell fires or outer darkness, which are both biblical pictures of hell. Humans send themselves there. Hell is a very sad place where there will be 'weeping and gnashing of teeth,' according to Jesus. The extreme sadness that exists there is because of people's missed opportunities to believe and because of their suffering over their separation from God's loving presence. The most important lesson is that we had better make sure that his love has rescued us from hell through Jesus."

The thought of hell gives me shivers.

Holly pursues him, "How do you know that he has rescued you, Bruce?"

"Well, here is a true incident in my life that faintly points to the risen Jesus' rescue in my life, one of many examples that I could describe besides his most important one when I was sixteen. After I experienced almost-daily migraines for more than five years in Canada, we moved to South Dakota on the Rosebud Reservation. For a year before I received Lakeview Church's call to be their pastor on the rolling plains of southern South Dakota near Nebraska, I had prayed daily that God would send me to a place where my migraines would no longer be a problem.

"Though the migraines continued a little less frequently, they were still too frequent for me until the doctor scheduled me for right-shoulder surgery in North Platte, Nebraska, a two-and-a-half hour drive south of us.

"During the previous summer, I had shared in prayer my anger at God that he had allowed my migraines along with my confession of my selfishness in expressing my self-centered feelings. I eventually received his gift of peace after many prayers. As a result, he enabled me to submit to his will to allow migraines in my life.

"However, I had eleven migraines in nine days leading up to the shoulder surgery, which surprisingly stopped my migraines for a whole week. Then I fell flat on my right shoulder, which was in a sling, while tripping over the top step of the ones leading up to the front door of our church. That fall triggered daily migraines again! That series of events couldn't have been a coincidence, as no events are."

I exclaim, "Incredible! What happened next?"

"I'm convinced that my risen Rescuer, Jesus, from my Father through the Spirit guided those events to answer my long-standing prayer for relief and to give me a final, non-medical relief from my migraines.

"Anyway, I prayed for God's guidance, and it came to me (I believe, from him) that I should start pressing a doorpost against my right shoulder to see if I could stop my migraines. Sure enough, when a debilitating headache started, I pressed my shoulder against a doorpost at the most painful place for ten to fifteen minutes. My 'doorpost therapy' caused pain in my shoulder, but not nearly as much as a major migraine with nausea. Wonder of wonders, my migraine stopped immediately as soon as I found the right place in my shoulder. A few minutes later, the migraine went away completely! I praise the Lord for his non-medical answer to my long-standing prayer.

"For two months, I worked on my shoulder with my painful, God-provided therapy ten or fifteen minutes a day. Amazingly, God has kept me free from medium and major migraines right up to the present! I believe that it was his guidance to give me a new lease on life!

"That amazing result is a tiny picture of God's rescue through Jesus by the Holy Spirit's power that will give all believers a place in heaven when they die and, later, a place in the new heaven and new earth with perfect bodies, when Jesus comes again. I eagerly look forward to that day!

"By the way, Joe and Holly, you're always welcome to come to our church on Sunday mornings at 10:00 A.M."

Our answering, two-minute, puzzled silence ends with my dramatic declaration with a glance at Holly, "We'll think about it!"

Holly answers, "We'll talk about it."

CHAPTER 48

Good news

As I sat next to Joe's hospital bed, waiting for him to wake up from surgery, I read an academic book by Frank Rees entitled *Wrestling With Doubt*. Eventually, my doubting friend opened his eyes and squinted at me. "How are ya doin', Bruce?"

"I'm doin' fine, Joe! My next question's a *little* more important at this moment. How are *you* doin', Joe?"

"I'm a little uncomfortable, but I'm doin' good otherwise."

The surgeon's entrance interrupted our profound discussion, "Mr. Smith, do you want privacy for our discussion?"

"No, Bruce is like family. Fire away!"

Dr. Wilson plunged right in, "I believe that our robotic system got all of the malignancy, which doesn't appear to have spread beyond the prostate. The nurse will give you my instructions for going home and for further treatment. But your condition is looking very *good*."

With the doctor's confident utterance of the word "good," Joe's family—Phil, Josephine, and Phyllis—arrived to visit their son and brother and to rejoice with Joe and me about the surgeon's good news. After a while the room became so full with Holly and other visitors that I exited with a good-bye to head home to our small far-eastern Iowa town.

Part Ten Questions:

1. What was your reaction to Joe's report of the rest of the trial? Explain.
2. What impressions of small-town people at the pool and at George's house do you get from this chapter? How fair are those descriptions to people in small towns?
3. Why do you think that the writer introduced the narrator's Bible discussion group now? Explain.
4. How has the author prepared you, the readers, for Joe's arrival at the Bible discussion group's meeting? How?

Extended Bible Study: Read Matthew 24 and 25. Look over the questions and answers that the group considered in this chapter. How satisfied are you that they covered those chapters with good biblical interpretation? What other questions and answers might they have considered about those passages? Time permitting, look at the other passages to which the group referred. Construct a sequence of the events at Jesus' Second Coming. What difference does the belief that Jesus will return make in your life? What difference should it make?

PART 11

How important is the church?

CHAPTER 49

New attenders

Holly and I edge through the front door of Bruce's high-peaked, steepled church. Suddenly, a greeter with a big smile puts out his hand to give us a hearty handshake. *He certainly is friendly.* Then, two other members inquire how we are until we enter the open, middle door to the auditorium. A friendly, grinning, young usher with a beard greets us with firm handshakes, a squeeze of my shoulder, and a hug for Holly. He leads us to a pew about a third of the way to the stage area. *This church certainly seems friendly.*

The church with a high, peaked ceiling reaching toward heaven looks particularly bright this Sunday morning with its light shining on the high eastern windows. Dominating the front is a large cross on the back wall. *That cross reminds me of Bruce's reference to Jesus' death. Was that event for me?* The pulpit is in the center of the stage three steps above the communion table, which is in the center at floor level.

The gray-haired minister, wearing a gray suit and a bright-blue tie, leaves the first row of pews to face us behind the pulpit, greets us with a reading from the Bible, and invites us to greet each other. Several people around us shake our hands and welcome us. *That welcome certainly feels good.* Then all of us remain standing to sing praises to God loudly as we use words and music projected on the wall on both sides of the stage. We then sit on padded pews to hear the choir's anthem, confess our sins, and hear God's pardon through Jesus' death as well as biblical instructions for our walk with him. The minister then prays for people's needs. We then rise to sing his praises again and sit to hear the Bible reading before the pastor's message.

The Bible passage and message are about the importance of gathering together in church for worship and mutual support based on Hebrews 10:24, 25: "And let us consider how we may spur one another on toward love and good deeds, not giving up meeting together, as some are in the habit of doing, but encouraging one another—and all the more as you see the Day approaching." *If God exists, he certainly planned the passage and message for both of us.*

The pastor, a middle-aged man with a ready smile and a booming, base voice, emphasizes the Bible's statement that Christians all need each other as the church and that we need God all of the time, especially in these tough times.

After the worship service in the church entrance, Bruce and Winnie say, "You're invited to our condo for lunch." and leave soon afterwards, as I joke with some church members, "We've got to stop meeting this way" with a wink and a grin. Our arrival at Bruce's condo results in my conversation with him in his basement surround-sound room as Holly talks with Winnie, while she prepares our lunch upstairs at the front of the condo.

I approach the subject of the pastor's message by asking, "Bruce, how can you go to church Sunday after Sunday with people who lead double lives? I saw at least six people rumored to have cheated others or led immoral lives."

"Easy, Joe. First of all, the important part is that you have heard gossip. You know how exaggerated stories can go around in a small town. Second, we're all sinners in church just as you and I are. Many of us are struggling with the sins in our lives as genuine Christians. Others are hypocrites unaware of their 'double lives,' as you put it. The head of the church is the risen Jesus with God the Father. In our tradition the human leaders of our church are the elders, who are responsible under Jesus to oversee the spiritual condition of the people in the church."

"But, Bruce, I don't understand why church is so important to you."

"O, I see. First, I find God there in his Word, the Bible. If the pastor didn't preach and teach God's Word in our church, I'd find another one that preached the Bible. Second, I find other Christians' support and love like our group that you're attending. Third, God calls all Christians in his Word to gather together one day in seven to worship him so that he can re-charge our spiritual 'batteries.' At the same time, he enables us to grow to be more like Jesus. I'm really enjoying sitting in the pew every Sunday soaking up God's Word without the stress of preaching God's Word.

"On the other hand, I did enjoy preaching God's Word for those twenty-seven years in the preaching ministry!...Joe, what do you get out of our worship service?"

"Well, I've been interested in the singing and sermons 'cause I'm trying to find your God. I'm not there yet, though."

CHAPTER 50

What's the point?

There was a cool pool, literally, waiting for us late Monday afternoon, resulting in an especially-bracing swim, as I swam alone my many lovely laps for God's gift of health. Halfway through my laps, I spied Joe limping slowly toward the hot-tub on the east side of the pool. When I finished my laps and settled into the spa, Joe greeted me as we both saw Holly jump uncharacteristically into the pool like a sleek bomb dropping from the sky ready to explode.

"How're ya doing, Joe?"

"Not so good, Bruce. I have a lot of pain and tiredness today."

"That's not good news, Joe."

He was ready with a shot over my bow, "I just don't understand what you see in going to church when there are so many sinners there."

"Yeah, there are a lot of sinners there, just like you and me."

"You're not a sinner, Bruce."

"I certainly am, Joe. I'm just like Paul, God's missionary, writer, and preacher, who founded many churches. He wrote, 'I'm the worst of sinners.' For the first sixteen years of my life I was what I call an 'ignorostic,' ignoring God. During the next seventeen years, I refused to talk about God except in safe places like Bible discussions, while God clearly calls all Christians to share God with others. Yeah, I'm a sinner, Joe. Remember that we discussed once before that sin is self-centeredness in our sinful nature, which is in me as well as all people. (I'm presently struggling with impatience about how long it's taking to publish my first book.) The difference between believers in the 3-in-1 God and unbelievers is that he gives believers faith and helps them fight those self-centered impulses of selfish pride.

"By contrast, unbelievers are controlled, not by that one only true God, but by the god of this world, the devil, along with his demons. As you read in the Book of Job, Satan is only allowed to attack believers as far as God permits. God is all-powerful! However, God enables us who submit to his power in Jesus by the Spirit's power gradually to make some progress in the lifelong battle against the devil, the sinful nature within us, and the tempting world around us.

"Those reasons are just some of all the considerations that prompt sinner-saint believers to gather together in God's church. We need to gain more and more of God's strength to fight in God's holy war against those evil forces within and all around us, not against people. God calls us to find a church that is centered on his Word, the Bible, and on him. I'm fighting in God's strength several bad, sinful qualities, not the least of which is selfish pride. Sorry, Joe; I'm going on and on."

"No, Bruce, I love to hear you talk, 'cause you're genuine. So many people say things that are meant to please the hearer. You speak from the heart."

"Thanks, Joe, for the compliment, but I just tell it as it is. As I previously told you, I used to say what I thought other people wanted to hear. However, God has taught me through many hard experiences that the only thing that counts in this life is to please him and *only* him. The result is that I pray every day for the filling of his Spirit and for his words to speak for that purpose. I'm thankful that he has made me more of a God-pleaser than a people-pleaser, partly through his Word in church."

Joe's skepticism reared its monster-head once again, "I still don't understand your attraction to church when so *many* imperfect people go there."

God made me ready to fight that unbelieving objection, "Well, Joe, the true church is something like a good basketball team."

"How's that, Bruce?"

I slayed one of Joe's skeptical monster-heads with experience from my basketball coaching, "You'll notice that the best teams are the ones that play together unselfishly as a team on offense and defense. The year when I coached seventh-grade basketball, my last year in teaching, was very enjoyable. I tried to teach the boys that if we were unselfish enough to pass the ball quickly to the hot shooter or the open guy, no matter who he was; if we helped each other stopping the ball on defense; and if we hustled as hard as we could, we would be competitive.

"The same thing is true in the team of the church. God helps us by the Holy Spirit to be more and more unselfish toward each other and the people that God sends to us. The result is God's blessing on us as Jesus' body."

"Wait a minute, Bruce. The church of believers is also Jesus' 'body'? Whatcha mean, preacher-man?"

I again laughed at Joe's face as it plunged into funny gyrations, "Yeah, Joe, the Bible describes the church in Ephesians chapter four and Romans 12 as being like a human body," as I pointed at mine. "The head is Jesus, as he directs all the movements of the members of the body by giving them the Holy Spirit's power. Jesus directs the rest of us as his body through his Word, especially as it's preached, discussed, and taught in his church.

"There are a lot of churches that say that they're Christian. But they, sadly, don't preach or teach the true Word of God or act at all the way God wants them to act, like the church that I grew up attending. They preached moralistic human stories rather than the Word of God. That's the reason I enjoy our church's preaching based squarely on the texts of the Bible and centered on the only true, 3-in-1 God."

At this point Holly entered the theological spa.

CHAPTER 51

Imperfect people

I laugh as I settle into the hot-tub, "Ha, I see that we are being biblical again today!"

Joe expresses his curiosity to Bruce, "How did your team do that season?"

"We were a small junior high school in Gurnee, Illinois, my hometown. I taught the guys not to argue with the referees and that I would take up the players' cause in a respectful discussion with the referees. I played all of my twenty-five players—that maneuver was a real trick since we only had four five-minute quarters!—in non-conference games. We lost all of those games. (I remember one game in which we lost 60 to 6 when we played a big junior high, but I remained resolved to play all of my guys so that all of them could experience the fun of basketball.)" *That game must have been embarrassing, but Bruce doesn't seem to be ashamed of such a drubbing. A lot of people would never mention it to anyone. Interesting!*

"However, I played our best fourteen players in conference games. We ended up with five wins and three losses while surviving a couple of tough two-point wins at other junior high schools in the process of winning a trophy for our second-place tie in the conference.

"On the other hand, we were involved in an eight-team tournament with seven big junior highs at the end of the season. During our first game we stayed close during the first half but were blown out in the second half to lose big. However, we won the sportsmanship trophy for that tournament. I was more excited for my guys when we won that award than for the winning season!"

Joe says, "Wow, that's great, Bruce!"

I exclaim, "I didn't know that you were a basketball coach, Bruce!"

.

"Yeah, I really enjoyed coaching the kids. I prayed before our games a simple prayer for all of the players' safety and for our best effort. In fact, I thought that I had invented the box-'n-one and triangle-'n-two defenses until I discovered later that someone else had used them before me. I know that God blessed me in that role. Coaching was the thing I missed most when I left teaching."

Bruce explains for my benefit, "Holly, I was trying to explain to Joe how the church is like a good basketball team."

"Yeah, I know that the church is supposed to be one with Jesus but that it often falls far short."

Bruce continues, "The three-Persons-in-one God is also a picture of the church. Individual believers are all one church with God the Father through Jesus as the church's head by the Holy Spirit's power."

Joe objects, "But how can you trust a bunch of sinners, some of whom are hypocrites?" *That's right, Bruce—how?*

Bruce expresses his faith, "No, Joe, I don't focus on them and their failings. I focus on the great, mysterious God who called them to trust him. I don't go to church for the people, first of all, but to re-focus on that amazing God. Second, I go because he calls me to fellowship on Sundays with him and with them. I belong to that Bible-discussion group for the same reason. I look beyond their sins to the Rescuer who has rescued many of them from their sins. After all, it's the people's responsibility what they do with God's Word." *Bruce has an interesting point-of-view. I wish I could look beyond the church's sins but to Jesus instead, but it's hard to do.*

"People will often let you down, but God will never let you down! Furthermore, I want to go to places where he reveals himself. The most important place is in a Bible-believing, Christ-centered church. I hope that you can find him there too, Holly and Joe."

I hope that I can too.

When Joe sits up on the hot-tub edge as Bruce's skin-puckering made him do the same, he agreed with Bruce, "Yeah, I hope so too. But what I can't figure out is why God—if he does exist—would be so interested in a bunch of sinners."

Bruce agrees, "I know, Joe. That mystery is one I can't figure out either. Why would God love and show his grace to accept a sinner like me? The amazing thing is that he loves the church of true sinner-saints."

CHAPTER 52

A vision

Bruce continues, "I'll give you an amazing, true example. In one of my churches, the leaders were thinking about a move to the north side from the south side of their city of 225,000 people. However, there was a lot of discussion because the church had always been on the south side of town. (In fact, the church's neighborhood was originally made up almost completely of church members.)

"Well, it was 5:00 A.M. on Monday, my day off, when I awoke with something like a dream but not a dream, because I forget dreams. This something-like-a-dream is just as vivid today as it was then."

Joe breaks in with as much excitement as he can muster, "What happened, Bruce?"

"Yeah, Bruce, what happened?" I echo Joe.

He continues with growing excitement in his voice, "Well, the last thing I wanted to do was to be awake at 5:00 A.M. on my day off, because I'm a late person! But this vision was in two parts. The first part was my view of the church with no one in it. There was a passageway between the church building and the parsonage next door that wasn't normally there. Parking places were all around the church and parsonage where the lawn was at that time.

"The next part of the vision was a vivid picture of our church members worshiping and having Sunday School in a school and its gym, while I somehow sensed that they were waiting to have their church building built on the northside of town. I awoke that Monday morning fully rested inspite of that vision or dream.

"The next Friday I dreamed about a message for our Ascension Day celebration the following Sunday morning that was entirely different from the one I had been preparing all week. As a result, I preached about the need for the people to turn away from sin in the light of Jesus' re-entry to heaven."

Because Joe and I hang on every word, Bruce continues with increasing awe, "The following December I had accepted a call to another church. In my parting message, I preached on Paul's 'thorn in the flesh' and the vision of his visit to the third heaven in 2 Corinthians 12. For the first time, I shared with the church God's vision given to me several months previously.

"After we moved from that church and city, I heard later that they bought an eighty-acre plot of land north of town and made plans to build a new church after they sold their building to a man who wanted to use it as a daycare and who let them stay several months. The people, many of whom had moved to farms a few miles north of the new plot of land, planned to build the new building and move into it directly from the old building.

"The event that still gives me goosebumps is that the construction took longer than they had planned so that they had to move into the Christian School gym while the new building was being finished!"

Wow! God may think that his church is important after all!

"Thus, God fulfilled the vision that he gave me! I heard later from my minister friend in that city that my experience had all the earmarks of a vision from God. Yes, God does care for his church. My experience was all to his credit!"

Joe and I stare at Bruce in great wonder for several minutes.

I slowly break the ensuing silence, "That's an amazing...true story,...Bruce!"

Maybe I should attend church regularly.

Bruce then quizzically comments to Joe, me, and no one in particular, "I wonder why people get turned off by the church. Maybe it's because they get distracted by people's faults instead of focusing on the great God of the true church."

CHAPTER 53

Fellowship

That Wednesday, Bruce's Bible-discussion group meets at Sally's house in her well-appointed living room with Joe and me again in punctual attendance. Volunteers read the passage to be discussed, Ephesians chapter four, before Sally opens with a short prayer for God's blessing on our discussion and fellowship. She then asks what we learned from the passage emphasizing the church's oneness in the three-Persons-in-one God.

Dependable, learned George pipes up, "I noticed that it's Paul's practical application of his teachings in the first three chapters. There, he said that God chose believers—his church—before he created anything and that God rescued believers from our stillborn, spiritual condition by making us alive to him through Jesus. The result is that we live for God by grace through faith with thankful good works. God chooses all believers to be one in his church, though we are from many cultures and races."

This passage tells me to attend and be active in church. I'm not sure I want to be involved, though, for fear that I will be disappointed again .

"Now, he gives us goals to work toward unity and maturity within that oneness through his chosen servants, God's appointed preachers and teachers."

Larry furthers the discussion, "I noticed in verses one through six that our oneness and fellowship should reflect God as the Trinity: 'There is one body and one [Holy] Spirit, just as you were called to one hope, when you were called: one Lord [Jesus], one faith, one baptism; one God and Father of all, who is over all and through all and in all.' I see there the Trinity and the church, with oneness in severalness, if that's a word," as he smirks with the rest of us.

Bruce comments, "It probably isn't a word, but we'll have to call *Webster's Dictionary* about it and give credit to you, Larry!" The group erupts in giggles.

However, Sally returns us to the passage at hand, "But what else did you notice about this chapter?"

Joe pipes up, "I noticed that Christ provides church leaders to prepare believers for growing as a body. We were discussing that idea the other day in the swimming-pool hot-tub. What does it mean to you folks that the church is a 'body'?"

Sally responds with an approving smile, "Joe, I think that it means just what we do as a group and what our church does every Sunday. We learn and fellowship around God's Word so that, as the passage says, we can grow from immature, childish Christians to mature, grown-up Christians. What do you people think is the difference?"

Winnie responds, "I know that children are born to be selfish, not innocent, little people who all need to be taught to center their lives on God, not on themselves. It's the same way in our Christian lives. We become Christians and have to grow from our inborn self-centeredness to God-centeredness. God has provided the church to guide us along that pathway."

Joe says as he points at Bruce, "You folks are just conspirators with Bruce. Your comments are just like his the other day at the pool. Did he put you up to it?" The group all laughs. *There's a deep joy here that I haven't experienced with any other group of people.*

Sally re-directs us one more time, "What do you think about the last part of the chapter, where Paul called us to live for God by speaking the truth in love without telling lies and doing away with our self-centered anger. God also wants us to stop stealing but instead to work to be able to give to the poor. He also calls us to stop speaking crude language, avoid grieving the Holy Spirit, and stop acting out our anger?"

Larry answers with a grin, "Those are *several* tall orders, if ya ask me!"

Everyone laughs with Larry. Semi-serious George answers Larry's observation, "They're several 'tall orders' for sinful humans in their own strength, but they're *short* orders for us sinful-but-saved Christians in God's strength!"

Fred chimes in with a wide grin, "Those 'tall orders' are sure a lot easier when we support each other and worship together as God's church!"

I would really enjoy getting to know these people better.

* * *

So Christ himself gave the apostles, the prophets, the evangelists, the pastors and teachers, to equip his people for works of service, so that the body of Christ may be built up until we all reach unity in the faith and in the knowledge of the Son of God and become mature, attaining to all the measure of the fullness of Christ.
(Ephesians 4:11-13)

* * *

Part Eleven Questions:

1. In your own words, state the reason the narrator gives that makes hell necessary? Explain.
2. What was God's solution to enable people to escape eternal punishment in hell? How does Joe show that he is the hot-tub comic? How appropriate are his jokes?
3. What is the narrator's explanation for the suffering of believers? For Job's suffering? Explain. How does that explanation help your faith?
4. What unponderable question does Joe ask? How does the narrator respond? How appropriate is his response? How is the narrator's growing friendly relationship with Joe a model for our relationships with unbelievers and other Christians?
5. How does the narrator testify to God's dramatic relief of his daily migraines as a picture of God's spiritual rescue of his life from hell? How effective is that example? Why? What other parallels could you draw between God's spiritual rescue and his rescue of the narrator from migraines? How did the narrator use that comparison to give Joe an important invitation? How many people do you know to whom you could give a similar invitation? Why don't we invite people? Explain.
6. The author was surprised when Holly showed up in his book and in the hot-tub. How did you respond to her appearance in this book? How appropriate to Joe's character is his response to Holly's appearance? What is Joe's response to Holly as a sports fan? As a Christian? Why?
7. How effective is the Iowa City Hospital scene to advance the plot and characters of this book? Why?

PART 12

How can God love us?

CHAPTER 54

Loving and forgiving?

After church let out on the following Sunday, a young couple of our church invited Holly and Joe to their house for lunch. The result was my impatient wait until Monday afternoon to ask them privately about their second experience in our church. Joe made his limping, slow entrance to the swimming-pool locker room as I was putting on my swimsuit. I greeted him like some long-lost granduncle with joy as I marched with my own small limp in my swimming attire to his locker, "Hey, Joe, how's it going?" and shook his hand, which had the strength of a wet mop.

"I'm still alive, Bruce. Say, that was an interesting sermon your preacher gave yesterday. I wonder how your God can love us the way the preacher said that he does. More to the point, how can we possibly love our enemies? That kind of love doesn't come to us naturally."

"No, God's love isn't human, since he is spirit, not flesh, as you already read in John chapter four. (However, Jesus is both flesh *and* spirit with his resurrection body.) God loves me amazingly, even though I'm a sinner and don't at all deserve that love, in two ways: As his created human beings he loves you and me, Joe. And he loves me as someone who trusts and follows only Jesus as my Rescuer and Ruler and as the only Road to my heavenly Father. He loves believers even though we're unworthy sinners and calls all of us to trust more and more in Jesus as God's only Path to heaven beyond death. When we receive Jesus into our lives and surrender our whole lives to him, we're assured that after we die we will be forever in his loving, heavenly *presence*. If you give your life to him, we can continue our conversations there, Joe!"

"Ya mean if I believe in your 3-in-1 God, I goin' to get *presents*?"

We headed toward the door leading to the pool, "I was usin' the word 'presence' with a '-ce' endin' as in 'with him and his power in heaven,' silly Joe. That kind of love of unworthy human creatures is not at all ordinary, selfish human love. That's the point that I've been making with you all along. God's *unselfish* love is so different from humans' *selfish* love that he *had* to have revealed himself in the Bible. No one could've thought him up, not even with their wildest imaginations. And that love flows into the lives of believers to enable us to love other unworthy people. On second thought, I guess that you do get 'presents' with '-ts'. Eternal life and Jesus are no slouches as God's free presents!"

Joe's serious, skeptical mood reared its ugly head as we neared the pool, "You mean, you can love Osama Bin Laden and Adolph Hitler?"

I stopped walking abruptly, "I know, Joe, that it's hard to imagine, but I believe with all my heart that God made both of those people and you too as his creatures. I leave the earthly and divine judgment that everyone has coming to them up to God, who made them. As a result, I can love them and you, since everyone's God's creation."

He stared at me with his eyes bugged out and his mouth wide open as he dove into the deep end as if I had gone off of it. However, Joe's stamina only lasted five minutes, when he emerged to sink slowly into the hot-tub.

In the hot, bubbling shallows, we continued our conversation. Holly joined us a few minutes later. Joe exclaimed to her with that same dumbfounded look, "Holly, Bruce claims that God and he could love Osama Bin Laden and Adolph Hitler! What do you think about that claim?"

Holly took a deep breath, peered at Joe with a gleam in her eye, and launched into her answer with her high-pitched voice, "Yeah, Joe, I don't think that I can love them either."

Joe stared at me as if I were a little coo-coo, "Well, Jesus—if he exists—has certainly sailed a curve ball right by my head when he tells me to love my enemies."

I replied, "I can only do it in his rescuing strength, Joe! That passage in Luke chapter six on which our pastor preached also gave Jesus' reason that God 'is kind to the ungrateful and wicked.' We were all born 'ungrateful and wicked,' but God is still kind to us. For example, he keeps us alive each day, gives us each breath that we breathe, and supplies us with each beat of our hearts—freely by grace.

"However, a time of judgment after we die will come, as the next passage says. If we haven't trusted in Jesus in this life, our souls will sadly be declared 'guilty' and sent to hell, a very sad place. But God will declare all believers who have trusted in Jesus 'not guilty'—justified—and send them to heaven to await their resurrection. The last part of John chapter three plainly describes both results of our actions. Sadly, many people who quote John 3:16 from that chapter ignore Jesus' warning after that verse about condemnation for unbelievers."

Holly chimed in, "It's really hard for me to believe that we must love the people that God loves because he is their Creator."

I responded, "There's another passage (Mathew 7) that says, 'Judge not, and you will not be judged. Do not condemn, and you will not be condemned.' We are called to leave the judging of people to God, who in the beginning made them like him, and love them instead."

Joe shook his ample head with a frown, "I don't know; it seems to me that we *can* judge and condemn notorious, public sinners like Bin Laden and Hitler."

I shook my head with a slight grin, "Well, Joe, we certainly can discern that those two people did horrible sins and pray for God's power to enable us to avoid the uncontrolled, self-centered rage of which they were obviously guilty.

"However, what if Hitler, who did horrible things to about twenty million people, including six million Jews, repented of those sins and turned to God for forgiveness just before he died. Jesus forgave the Roman soldiers and Jewish leaders who killed him, even while he was hanging on the cross. Even though they committed a sinful action that was probably worse than any other sin ever committed. By that amazing act, he showed his heavenly Father's love for all of his human creatures in praying that his Father would postpone his judgment of them so that they could turn away from their sinfulness.

"On the other hand, the Bible says that we'll all appear before his throne and receive his verdict of 'guilty' or 'not guilty,' depending on whether or not we've accepted his Son as our Rescuer and Ruler. God is incredibly patient with humans during this life. On the other hand, he *allows* bad things to happen in their lives to *call* them to *trust* him and to *change* their actions to follow him and their thinking to his way of thinking in the Bible. Joe, just think back over all the traumatic events that God has allowed in your life. I believe that he is using all of them to call you to believe in him."

Joe was still shaking his head, "Well, your God is just so different from my human experience."

I replied with a lowered voice, "Yeah, he definitely is, but that difference shows that he is truly God." After a pause I whispered, "I know that it's hard for you to forgive *certain* people, Joe."

Holly answered as if she were confessing to a priest, "I hope that God will forgive and love me. However, I also have trouble forgiving certain people. Because I can't stop judging them on my own, I guess that I need God's power to forgive them."

I looked triumphantly at both Holly and Joe and declared, "Exactly! That kind of forgiveness and love couldn't have come from the human mind. Therefore, the early church could not have thought up or corrupted the New Testament, the way certain people, including some Muslims, have said. If they had thought it up or manipulated it, most of the passages never would have been written, especially Luke chapter six, where Jesus said that we should love our enemies. The Bible *had* to have come from God!"

CHAPTER 55

Unconditional love

Our church Bible-discussion group met the following Wednesday at George's house to discuss the last chapter of Jesus' Sermon on the Mount, Matthew 7, as we all sat in a circle at one end of George's cavernous, muted-yellow living room. After George opened with prayer and volunteers read the chapter, George prompted the discussion, "How can we get the judging 'plank' out of our own eyes in order to see clearly not to judge others, but instead to help them with the sinful sawdust in their eyes?"

I answered eagerly with one word, "Confession."

Sally confessed slowly, "I'm afraid...that I tend to judge...or condemn others...for their public sins."

George laid on us the tough question, "Why do you suppose that Jesus made a special commandment that we aren't supposed to judge and condemn others?"

Joe, who was resting with a couple of pillows against the left edge of George's long, gold, comfortable couch, said slowly, "Because of his claim...that his Father is the only Judge,...loving and yet just."

All of us paused in approving shock at Joe's answer until George asked, "If God the Father is loving *and* just, why should we withhold judgment and condemnation of other people?"

After another pause I answered, "Because he will judge everyone perfectly at the Final Judgment. He shows tough and tender love toward those who believe in him.

"To give you an example of his tough and tender love toward me in my life, he showed his tough love by allowing me to be born under my parents' cloud of stress over my brother Bobby's sickness. Their struggle, when I was in my mother's womb, ended in his death from leukemia when I was two-and-a-half months old.

"Bobby was the second child of four children. Much later our second child of four children, Keith, also died from leukemia at 4½ years old, an extremely stressful time in our lives. It was God's tough love to allow that traumatic time in our lives in order for him to draw close to us in my time of rebellion against his call to the ministry. Almost four years later he renewed his call in no uncertain terms, after changing my heart, and provided the means to make my time at seminary possible."

George broke the ensuing silence, "Thanks, Bruce, for your testimony. Does anyone else have other experiences to share?"

Larry, who had been quiet to this point, piped up eagerly, "Yeah, I was an angry, rebellious young man while I was in my twenties as part of the 'lost generation' 'cause I judged and condemned older adults for their hypocrisy and—to me—obvious sins. However, God disciplined me, as our Father should, by allowing me to lose my job.

"He then showed me his grace by enabling me to go back to school in Chicago and begin volunteering for an inner-city mission. It was there that I discovered how incredibly blessed I was growing up in a Christian home and how I was being ungrateful for those experiences revealing his love. He also enabled me with that same love to see my own selfish anger as my sin against others *and* God. I began confessing it, and he took away my angry judgment! Praise God!"

Sally said slowly, "Thank you, Larry. It seems to me that when God the Father gave his willing Son to die on the cross, he punished Jesus in order to show his grace to us who trust in Jesus' death for our forgiveness. I've come to learn that we *rightly* earned God's anger that was *instead* satisfied for us by Jesus' death on the cross. That unselfish action as the evidence of his love for us is the reason for the Bible's statement that we are justified or forgiven fully the moment that we believe in Jesus."

Joe's skepticism reasserted itself with his comment, "That kind of love seems so out of this world, given all that's happening around us. It's a rare and almost non-existent kind of love."

George charged into Joe's skepticism, "Joe, the human race has rejected God's unconditional love by trying to earn their false gods' love by being good. We can't earn the true God's love. All we need to do is to receive our Father's love through Jesus and let the Spirit take over our lives. It's because God's kind of unconditional love is so rare in humans and condemning is so common that people have rejected God's great love."

Joe answered George's faith with his doubt, "Do you believe in the 3-in-1 God's love that Bruce talks about?"

"Yes, Joe, I believe in the God of the Bible, who showed himself there as three Persons in one God or the Trinity, because no human could've thought him or his amazing love up, the way that Bruce has said. I believe because of the eyewitnesses' testimonies to their faith in Jesus even when they faced death. God's no-strings-attached love cannot be found very often among humans—maybe a little more often than hen's teeth. When you do find it—and I do find it in the church—it's the same God's free, miraculous gift!"

Joe responded with his familiar theme, "It's all so unbelievable."

CHAPTER 56

The source of human talent

The following Tuesday Joe, Holly, and Winnie joined me in my W'nW room, where I watch and write, to watch a Bulls-versus-Boston-Celtics basketball game. The Chicago Bulls beat the former NBA champs 127 to 121.

After the game Joe exclaimed excitedly, "What a great game! I didn't think that the Bulls had a chance to win, since they are fighting for their playoff lives, whereas the Celtics are shoo-ins for the playoffs. That game sure gives the Bulls a boost in their confidence. If they can beat the Celtics, they can beat any team!"

Holly chimed in, "Yeah, God gave both teams a lot of talent!"

I echoed her comment, "He sure did! I believe that human talent and the ability to use it are both sure evidences of his love for his creatures!"

When Winnie and Holly exited to retrieve refreshments, I took the opportunity to ask Joe, "What's the latest on the medical front?"

He answered wearily while resting on pillows against the right-corner of our blue, stuffed sofa, "There's not much news. I'm waiting for the results of my tests."

"Well, you can be thankful that you aren't part of the 'free' medical system in Canada, where waiting a long time for almost anything medical is a way of life. However, our American medical system has its own problems, all caused by human sin. God is greater than human weaknesses and can break through the system to use medical means to help you, Joe, because he loves you."

"I sure hope he does—if he exists, that is," Joe responded with a mixture of hope and skepticism.

* * *

When [Israel] came to Marah, they could not drink its water because it was bitter. (That is why the place is called Marah.) So the people grumbled against Moses, saying, "What are we to drink?" Then Moses cried out to the LORD, and the LORD showed him a piece of wood. He threw it into the water, and the water became sweet. There the LORD issued a ruling and instruction for them and put them to the test. He said, "If you listen to the LORD your God and do what is right in his eyes, if you pay attention to his commands and keep all his decrees, I will not bring on you any of the diseases I brought on the Egyptians, for I am the LORD, who heals you."

(Exodus 15:23-26)

* * *

Part Twelve Questions:

1. Why was Joe skeptical about attending church? How understandable is that skepticism? Explain.
2. Why does the narrator compare the church to a basketball team? How convincing is that comparison?
3. What dramatic, true example does the narrator give of God's concern for and guidance of his church? How does the truth of that event and its fulfillment affect your faith?
4. Why do you think that people get turned off by the church? How can we prevent ourselves from getting discouraged by the church?
5. How does the Bible-discussion group compare God as Trinity to the church, based on Ephesians chapter four? What are the points of comparison between a human body and the church, according to Paul? Give some examples of the difference between childish and mature Christians without giving any names.
6. What is Fred's observation about how we can make progress in spiritual growth? Why is being part of a Bible discussion group important for our spiritual growth?

PART 13

What do believers have to do with Abraham?

CHAPTER 57

New Things

After the church's hour-long worship ends one Sunday morning, a sudden circle forms around Holly and me as it had on other Sundays after we left the auditorium. Bruce works his friendly way through the crowd to ask us over to Sunday lunch afterwards. I accept his invitation with a flourish of gratitude, "Thank you so much, Sir!" as I bow toward him, while the crowd around me giggles.

Fifteen minutes after they arrive at their condo on Straight Court, I maneuver my sport sedan into the short, dead-end street between the four-condo, one-story buildings on either side of the street to park in the parking spaces at the end of their half-block-long, quiet street. Bruce welcomes us into their warm-muffin-colored living room on the main floor. While Holly joins Winnie in the kitchen, he asks the inevitable question as we sit on the brown recliner and couch, "Joe, how was church for you this morning?"

I reply, "I liked it. Your people's...singing is...loud!"

Bruce laughs at my comical facial gyrations and shoots back, "Yeah, that's a tradition in the Christian Reformed Church. Singing loudly is how we express our joy in Jesus."

"That message about the covenant of circumcision was interesting. I heard from my Baptist friend in high school that the Old Testament, the covenant with Abraham, and the law given to Israel only apply to Jews, not to Christians. I know, from our previous conversations and what your minister said this morning, that you disagree with my friend, who said that he was a New Testament Christian. Why, Bruce?"

"I'm very thankful for the preaching of the Good News in the Baptist church that we attended when God rescued me. They preached the Old Testament as if it was just for the Jews. However, it's important to know, Joe, that the covenant is a less important belief than the basic beliefs that we have already discussed, upon which the Baptists and we agree wholeheartedly. For example, we all believe the existence of God as our Creator and Rescuer as three Persons in one God, Jesus as both God and human, and the Bible as God's Word.

"However, we do agree to disagree about the covenant God made with Abraham. I believe on the basis of Romans 4, 1 Peter 2, and Galatians 3 that all Christians of all nations are spiritual 'children' of Abraham. Those passages, especially Galatians 3, say that the promises of God's covenant are for all Christians, who are Abraham's spiritual 'descendents' because they have the same kind of faith as Abraham.

"On the other hand, God's promise to Abraham of the Land of Canaan has now taken the new-covenant form of his promise of the *whole new earth*, which Jesus will create out of this old earth and give to all believers when he returns."

I wonder what Holly's doing in the kitchen. I really like that woman.

My eye contact begins to wander as I say, "How's that?"

Bruce illustrates his point about the old and new covenant, "For example, the Ten Commandments say, 'You shall not murder.'"

"Yeah, I remember that commandment from Sunday School."

"Well, the basic idea continues now concerning God's desire for us to preserve life. However, Jesus made the law much deeper in his Sermon on the Mount by saying that we shouldn't hate or have self-centered anger toward each other, whether or not we physically murder anyone. If we do, we are murdering them. Negative gossip would be a small-town example of murder." *If that's so, small-town people murder people often.* "That idea continues into the new covenant, while the Israelite form (for example, the death penalty for children who curse their parents) disappeared.

"One time I was part of a conversation during which one person described a small-town man's greed. I observed, 'Now, tell me something good about that man' in order to make the picture balanced, since there's good and bad in all of us.

"An even better example is the law's command that Israel shouldn't harvest their fields all the way to the edges for the sake of the poor in that agricultural nation. But the new covenant is for an international church with the continuing principle of taking care of the poor. As a result, Christian farmers no longer have to harvest their fields in the same way as the Old Testament farmers were supposed to do, because the outward form of the same covenant has changed. Instead, we give a tenth and more of our income with our thankfulness for God's gift of income to the church and other Christian causes, partly to help the poor.

"Another example is the Sabbath Day. Some Christians still believe that we should worship on Saturday because of the literal form of the commandment. However, I believe that God changed the literal form of the old-covenant rules (called the 'letter of the law') about the seventh day (the Sabbath) for the new-covenant church. Thus, the early church continued to worship and rest on one day in seven, which was the main idea of the commandment. But instead, they observed Sunday, because it's the day that Jesus rose from the dead. They could've chosen any day—say, Wednesday—but they chose to celebrate Jesus' resurrection on the first day of each week with rest and worship, which were the basic principles of the old Sabbath Day, which is now called the Lord's Day."

"I see," I respond, as I suddenly understand. "The form of Israel's law was changed by Jesus, but the principles or ideas behind the church's law continued on for his followers. You told me about how God—if he does exist—helped you overcome lust. How does that new-found ability relate to the new covenant?"

"That's a great question! Well, God said in the Ten Commandments, 'You shall not commit adultery' for the nation of Israel. Under the new covenant for the church, the principle of having sex only within marriage and preserving that relationship continues. However, Jesus said that lusting after people who aren't our spouses is also adultery, whether or not we actually go to bed with them." *Here I thought that not going to bed with a woman was enough to avoid committing adultery. I've been guilty a lot of breaking that rule.*

"On the other hand, Jesus' death gives believers the verdict of 'not guilty' for all their sins. In addition, his resurrection gives us his unlimited power by the Holy Spirit to overcome the comparatively-puny power of that sin." *If I can believe in him, I hope he'll forgive me and help me do better.*

Winnie interrupts our conversation with the announcement of lunch. Our simple meal is preceded by Bruce's thanks for God's gift of food and by his prayer for his gift of health through God's blessing on the food. As we eat chicken noodle soup and ham sandwiches at the dining room table, I ask him, "Bruce, you prayed that your God would bless the food so that we can have health. What if your God doesn't answer your prayer and we get sick?"

He pauses briefly and then answers, "Joe, God is all-powerful and we are very weak. That insight is an understanding that I have gained from my pain! He sees the big picture, whereas my knowledge is very small. But he has promised always to bring good out of every situation for believers. If I pray for health this noon and then drop dead an hour later, God will bring about, during my funeral and afterwards, spiritual growth for true Christians and maybe even rescue some unbelievers. Believers are all in a new-covenant relationship with him, whether they know it or not. My plans are often different from God's plans.

"However, I know that if I die after praying for health, I will be totally healthy and happy in heaven. There, all believers who have died will await our souls' coming back with Jesus at his return. Then our souls will be joined with our new resurrection bodies. Our risen bodies will be these old, weak, painful ones that will crumble into dust in the grave. Then, they will become new, painless, always-healthy, and perfect at Jesus' return!"

I observe, "Ah, I see! Believers' new-covenant bodies will be these old bodies made perfect—different and yet similar like the new covenant! I wish I could believe in that future event."

"You will, my friend, you will!"

I gaze at my dwindling soup, "I hope so."

Winnie says, "We've been praying for both of you daily."

CHAPTER 58

Abraham, where are you?

Again, on late Monday afternoon our "hot-tub theology group" meets after our umpteenth victory over the watery depths. Bruce greets Joe and me, who enter the spa almost simultaneously, with his cheery, "Hi, how are you two today?"

I respond with my usual "OK."

Joe says with a grin, "Rotten!"

Bruce asks Joe with a flickering grin, "How rotten are you?"

He answers slowly with a wry, Tony-the-Tiger grin, "I feel gr-r-eat!"

Then Bruce asks as he leans forward, "Really, what's happening, Joe?"

"Well, if you must know, I've been having a lot of pain lately—here in my upper abdomen." *O, no, Joe!*

Bruce empathizes with a frown, "That's horrible news, Joe!"

I echo Bruce's empathy for Joe, "Yeah, it sure is. What does your doctor say?"

Joe descends into a melancholy mood, "My doctor is sending me to Mayo Clinic in Rochester, way up northwest in Minnesota, in a couple weeks to diagnose and treat my condition."

Bruce and I grin at Joe's joke about our northwestern neighbor and exclaim almost in unison, "I hope Mayo gets rid of that cancer!" Bruce promises him that he would pray for him. Bruce adds, "God provided Mayo as a great place for me to go for the diagnosis of my rare, hereditary nerve disease that's giving me numbness and making my pain in my legs and feet very strong!"

Changing the subject, Bruce asks me, "What did you think about the message yesterday, Holly?"

"I thought that it was interesting. It was a new idea to me that Christians are children of Abraham and part of the covenant that God made with him. I was going to ask you, Bruce, how that covenant could apply to us when Joe shared with me your explanation about the new covenant. It makes sense. However, how can the church be part of the new form of the covenant made with Abraham when it commits obvious sins?"

Bruce responds, "That's an excellent question, Holly! God has rescued through Jesus the church of believers, but just as in the Old Testament or Covenant, the visible church includes unbelieving hypocrites and weak Christians. Our self-centered will still influences all believers. God came to Abraham to rescue him and many of his descendents from the control of sin and Satan. In Genesis seventeen he came back to him to renew that covenant by repeating his promises of a son, even though Abraham was 99 years old and Sarah was 89.

"He also required circumcision for Abraham and his household, a ceremony which was Abraham's side of God's covenant. The meaning of that ceremony was the cutting away of self-centered sin in Israel's lives. Of course, it was replaced by baptism under the new covenant. The meaning of that New Testament word translated 'new' in 'new covenant' is 'new and improved' unlike the word for 'new' translated 'baby,' which is a different word that means 'brand-new'."

As Joe and I ride away from Bruce and Winnie's condo on Straight Court, Joe turns to me and kisses me lightly on the cheek. I turn to him and inquire, "What's that kiss for?"

He answers, "Nothing in particular." *I feel as if I'm falling for this guy.*

CHAPTER 59

Free love

Bruce's church Bible-discussion group meets at his condo the following Wednesday night with Joe and me in prompt attendance to discuss Luke chapter twenty-three, the first thirty-five verses. When the group comes to Luke's description of Jesus' celebration of the Passover with his followers and Jesus' beginning of the Lord's Supper, someone observes that Jesus thanked God the Father for the bread and cup. He also declared that the bread and cup were his body and blood of the 'new covenant' in verse twenty. Bruce asks us, "What strikes you about their Passover celebration?"

Sally speaks up after a brief pause, "Well, it seems to me that they had to be grieving 'cause Jesus had predicted to the disciples several times that he was going to be killed. Now he predicted that one of them will betray him and compares the bread and wine to his body and blood!"

Larry agrees, "Yeah, that time had to be hard for the disciples. Later they would be thankful that the Father forgave their desertion from Jesus that same night. He also forgave their denial that they ever knew Jesus. That fact shows me that God's grace flows to me through Jesus' death for me."

Joe says, "I notice Jesus' statement that the cup contained 'the blood of the new covenant.' What do you think he meant by that statement?"

George speaks up confidently, "I think that he meant that the fruit of the vine—the wine—was red like his blood, which was going to be shed like the blood of Old Testament animal sacrifices for believers' forgiveness."

Fred observes with his usual quiet insight, "It's interesting to me that Luke's account adds the word *new* to emphasize the covenant's newness, whereas my Bible study guide says that Matthew and Mark leave out the word *new* to emphasize the fact that the covenant continues on."

Comic Larry says with a wide grin, "Very good point, Fred! Does anyone have a hat for us to pass? Maybe we can collect money to send you to seminary!" All of us had a good laugh.

Bruce responds with awe in his voice, "Just imagine a holy and perfect God who is our all-powerful Creator coming to earth in Jesus to confirm a new form of the relationship that he made with Israel under the old covenant. The fact that he made that personal relationship with sinful me and with all believers, by way of his freely-given love, is what blows my mind away. No human minds could've come up with that idea!"

That's it! God came in Jesus to rescue me, even me! I no longer have to figure God out or hold against him the church's sins. I believe!

I interrupt the discussion to announce, "For the first time it all makes sense. God has broken through my anger at the church with his grace. The Bible has to be God's Word. I now believe in him!"

Bruce exclaims, "Praise the Lord! I'm thankful, Holly!" The group erupts in a spontaneous prayer of thanksgiving for God's miracle of the new birth in my life.

As we return to our discussion, my friend Joe pipes up, "I know from our discussions, Bruce, that your God's free love isn't exactly like the kind that they talked about back in the late '60s and early '70s!" A burst of laughter ensued.

During prayer time Joe asks the group to pray for him starting now and when he went "way up north" to get treatment at Mayo Clinic. After we eagerly pray for the group's needs and continue to thank the Lord for my experience, Bruce asks Joe, "Joe, is there anything that we as a group can do for you?"

He responds by thanking us for our prayers, "Just pray! Your prayers certainly can't hurt and maybe will help me." *My Father, be with Joe!*

CHAPTER 60

Little differences

On the following Friday evening, Winnie and I went out to eat according to our usual custom at the local Greasy Spoon Grille. As we entered the restaurant—a favorite eating place for retired people—the middle-aged, graying woman in charge of seating us led us past Joe and Holly's booth. They hailed us, as one would greet long-lost buddies, "Come, have dinner with us. We just arrived too!". Of course, we couldn't say "no" to their friendly offer.

During dinner Holly spoke to me, "Bruce, what God did for me the other night was amazing. He broke through my bitterness at people, especially abusive priests and those who covered up their abuse, and made me able to leave them in God's hands as their Judge."

I responded as I attacked a large piece of broiled catfish, "I'm grateful for his powerful work in your life, Holly. Your experience is a great example of the new covenant. You're still the same person but made new in Jesus. A lot of people think that when they see the word 'new' in the *New* Testament, it means 'completely different.' Of course, the Greek word that is used in the phrases 'new covenant (or testament), new earth, new heaven, and new Jerusalem' means 'new in quality' and 'new and improved' like a new and improved dish-washing liquid unlike the brand-newness (if that's a word) of a baby, for instance.

"As a result, Reformed believers interpret the Bible to mean that the same covenant with Abraham is 'new and improved,' because it's established inwardly with believers, as God just did with you. Incidentally, we don't believe that baptismal water saves a person. Instead, it's a sign of God's welcome to the covenant community and of his promise to bless the parents as they raise the child to follow God's ways, similar to the idea of God's sign of circumcision. Other groups believe that baptismal water rescues a baby or should be used for adults who come to believe.

"Inspite of the little differences among Christian groups, we all believe that Jesus came to give us the new birth to wash us clean from our sins, an action shown by water baptism.

"That action is also very different from the non-Christian groups' distant or close gods, who demand our obedience in order to gain their love. That difference makes me a Christian, because the human imagination couldn't have come up with the Bible's beliefs!"

Joe piped up between gulps of a reuben sandwich in his nasal, comedic voice like Gomer Pyle, "Well-said, preacher-man!"

* * *

> Peter replied, "Repent and be baptized, everyone of you, in the name of Jesus Christ for the forgiveness of your sins. And you will receive the gift of the Holy Spirit. The promise is for you and your children and for all who are far off—for all whom the Lord our God will call."
>
> (Acts 2:38,39)

Part Thirteen Discussion Questions:

1. How can Holly and the narrator love Osama Bin Laden and Adolph Hitler, according to the narrator? How can you love them and your more-immediate enemies?
2. What are Holly's reasons for loving her enemies? For what two reasons does Joe resist the idea of loving public sinners?
3. What do you think about the narrator's idea that the Bible had to have come from the God who is revealed there, because its ideas about that God are very different from the human mind and experience? How does that idea, repeated several times in this book, affect your faith in the God of the Bible? Why?
4. How did God show his tough and tender love to the narrator? How has he shown both kinds of love in your life?
5. According to Sally, what event was the evidence of God's love for us? How does that event affect your life now?
6. How is a basketball game related to God's love? Give an example of God's unconditional love shown in the world around you. How is his love clear in your life?

PART 14

How do divine and human plans work together?

CHAPTER 61

Sad Story

It is a month later in early September, as Holly and Bruce are lounging languidly in the hot-tub at the pool, when I suddenly make my tired entrance as only I can do with an over-exaggerated, slow wave high in the air and a tiny skip and a jump. They wait, while fidgeting, on the edge of the hot-tub for me to finish my shortened number of laps until I enter the hot-tub with my heavy breathing, limp, and exaggerated but sincere greeting, "Hi, folks! It's great to see ya!"

They greet me in unison, "Hi, Joe!" take turns hugging my wet, thinner body, as I settle into the steaming water. Noticing my yellow eyes, Bruce asks, "How did your time at Mayo Clinic go?"

I sit up straight in the hot-tub and reply, "Those great people were very thorough!"

Bruce agrees, "Yeah, that was my experience there too! What did you find out, Joe? We've been waiting impatiently for your return."

I smirk at Bruce, "I was in your church Sunday but didn't see you."

His surprised response was, "I didn't see you either, and I always look for you."

I chuckle, "Well, I came a little late, sat in the back with the little ones, and left right away at the end of the service."

"No wonder."

I divulge, "Mayo found out that I have at least one cancerous tumor—there's a big, long name for it—in my pancreas! It turns out that the kind of cancer I have is a very aggressive kind. I have only a few months to live...." My voice becomes fainter and fainter as I speak with tears creeping down my cheeks.

All of us sit in those steaming shallows in stunned silence for several seconds until Holly's mumbled words slash the dense silence as with a sword, "I'm stunned to hear your horrible news, Joe! What can we do?"

I pause what seems like an eternity but then answer raspily in the same tone that I did when Bruce first met me, "I don't know...what you can...do…other than pray."

After another solemn pause, I change the subject, "Say, I've been thinking about something your pastor said Sunday. Maybe I heard him wrong, but I thought that he said that God has a plan for everything that happens, causing good things to happen for believers and helping them through bad times. He also permits bad things to happen for unbelievers to bring about changes in their lives. Did I hear him right?"

Bruce recovers enough from his shock at my revelation to stumble through a reply, "That's pretty much...what he said,...when he was preaching on...Joseph's life in Genesis."

I shoot back at him with my piercing, angry arrow-question, "Then, how can I believe in your God when he has permitted me to get terminal cancer?!"

Holly deflects my skeptical shot back to me, "Joe, as you know, I've come to accept God's grace recently. God's love is mysterious, but it *is* his love that calls you to trust in him, no matter what he permits in your life.

"I've read that passage, and it seems to me that Joseph could forgive his brothers for selling him into many years of slavery because of God's larger, loving purpose to save their whole family and many other people besides them. Of course, he allowed and used Joseph's brothers' jealousy and anger, for which they were guilty and because of which they sold Joseph into slavery. On the other hand, he amazingly blessed Joseph as he rose from slavery and prison to become the second ruler in Egypt.

"Most of all, God gave him the ability to forgive his brothers *and* God. God's loving purposes are much larger than our shortsighted view of life. God is *not in the least* to blame for your cancer, Joe. Instead he has some great plan for you during these last few months!" she sputtered between her streaming tears.

I wish that I could believe in the God of Bruce and Holly.

I field Holly's line-drive explanation and throw it angrily back at both of them, "I feel like a puppet on strings, that is, if your God is real. I'm still not sure that I can believe in a God who pulls the strings to allow so much heartache!"

We sit there stunned by my situation until Bruce shares his hopeful denial, "I can understand your anger, but maybe Mayo is wrong."

However, Bruce makes one more observation after he pauses, "Certainly, the only true God has his plan for everything that happens in his creation. However, humans are also fully responsible for their rebellion against him ever since Adam, the result of which is cancer, other sicknesses, and death. *Both* are true: God's loving plan for all events *and* humans' full responsibility for all of their sins. For example, take Jesus' death on the cross."

A gleam returns to my eye, as I interrupt with a grin, "Where should I take it?"

Bruce grins as he continues, unperturbed, "Into your heart, Joe….As far as the one, only true God is concerned, the Father sent Jesus, who was more than willing to come to earth to be born in a stable on Christmas as the Father's unique Son. He then lived a perfect life—that we can never live—as the God-man. He suffered while carrying the extremely-heavy weight of our sins his whole life. He died willingly and triumphantly as the Winner-seeming-to-be-a-loser who substituted himself for us who trust in him. Then, he rose on the third day to give believers victory over death. All of those events involve God's perfect plan from beginning to end."

Did he do all of those actions for me?

"On the other hand, the people who sent Jesus to the cross because of their jealousy and hatred similar to the selfishness of Joseph's brothers were fully responsible for their sins against him. I believe that he is calling you, Joe, with the many, very hard experiences in your life and through his Word, to trust in Jesus to give you that same victory that all believers have now—as you saw Holly have—and will experience perfectly in heaven when they die. When Jesus returns, he will give true believers their resurrection bodies in the new universe. There won't be any cancer, pain, or death then! All you need to do is accept Jesus' life, death, and resurrection as the way to God as your Father, as Holly did! Of course, you can believe or not believe as you wish.

"There's a song entitled 'There Is None Like You' by Schrader that we heard someone sing recently in church. It expresses the biblical truth that the God of the Bible is unique compared to all the false gods developed by the human mind. That fact alone demonstrates that he revealed himself in the Bible. The refrain of that song says, 'There is none like you, no one else can touch my heart like you do. I could search for all eternity through and find there is none like you.' The mystery of God's plan and our responsibility in the Bible, along with God's mysterious nature described there, show to me its inspiration."

Holly's impishness asserts itself, "Sing that song for us, Bruce!"

I decline with a grin, "No way, Holly, I haven't been a good singer for over half a century, since my voice changed. A really good friend, who is an excellent singer, sat next to me in church one Sunday and said, afterwards, that I was an 'undeveloped tenor.'

"Joe, the proof of God's uniqueness along with the fact of Jesus' resurrection shows that God is real and Jesus is the God-man as the only way to know the Father. If you receive him into your life, Joe, we can continue our conversations beyond death!"

Holly joins in, "Well said, fellow believer!"

I lapse into my skeptical silence for several seconds but then come out of it to proclaim, "I'll think about it. If God does exist, I know what the Bible says and what he's done in your lives. Either those ideas and experiences are a series of coincidences due to luck or they're God's truth. I don't know which approach is true yet." *God, help me have faith in you.*

CHAPTER 62

Helpful discussion

The Bible-discussion-support group meets again the next evening in early September at a new member's house, as Holly and I arrive fifteen minutes early. Mike, the new host, opens with prayer. A volunteer reads Acts 4:1-22, the description of Peter and John's arrest by the group of religious leaders, the Sanhedrin, who had also condemned Jesus to a criminal's death. They arrested the two disciples because God—if he does exist—may have used Peter to heal a man who was lame from birth and because Peter had preached that Jesus rose from the dead.

Inspite of the peril of possible death at the hands of the religious leaders, Peter nevertheless claimed that God had healed the cripple through him "by the name of Jesus Christ of Nazareth, whom you killed, but whom God raised from the dead" (Acts 4:10). Then, he made an even more amazing claim, "Salvation is found in no one else, for there is no other name given under heaven by which we must be saved" (verse 12). In response, the Sanhedrin ordered Peter and John not to preach in the name of Jesus and let them go, since the healed man, who had been a lame beggar at the temple's gate, was present and because the crowds were praising God for his healing. Peter answered them courageously, "Which is right in God's eyes: to listen to you or to him?...As for us, we cannot stop speaking about what we have seen and heard."

Mike then asks, "What impresses you most about this passage?"

Sally answers, "It's Peter and John's amazing 'backbone' to speak about Jesus, not only to the crowds but to the same people who crucified Jesus and who could have killed them. Their courage in the face of possible torture and death shows me that Jesus rose from the dead. If they had made up their claim or had imagined that they had seen Jesus alive from the tomb, they certainly would have taken back that claim because of the Sanhedrin's threats!"

Larry asks, "How can we have the same kind of courage to speak for Jesus?"

Everyone sits silently in Mike's living room until Fred, who seldom joins the discussion, speaks up, "Maybe we can pray for the filling of the Holy Spirit and the words to speak every day. I think that we need to surrender more and more to Jesus' control every day."

Everyone nods in silent agreement until I observe with my usual skepticism, "Peter's claim that Jesus is the only way to God seems to me to be a little narrow."

Our group-scholar, George, answers my statement, "Joe, God, who is described in the Bible as knowing when the hairs on our heads fall off and also letting humans go their own way, could never have been made up by the human psyche.

"Furthermore, Jesus himself said to his followers that he is the only way to God the Father. As a result, we *have* to accept him as our Redeemer in order to be saved from our sins. On top of that, John—himself one of the eyewitnesses to Jesus' ministry, death, and resurrection—wrote down Jesus' words in his gospel and also heard Peter preach to the Sanhedrin in Acts. I believe God's eyewitnesses because of their courage. Therefore, I believe Jesus' claim."

I respond as I prop my head up with a pillow, "I'm still pondering those same ideas that Bruce has shared with me."

We then read the rest of Acts chapter four, in which the church praised God for his creative power in making everything. They also quoted David's Psalm two, which described earthly humans' futile attempts to oppose God. In their prayer they then applied Psalm two to their situation in verse 27, "Indeed Herod and Pontius Pilate met together with the Gentiles and people of Israel in this city to conspire against your holy servant Jesus, whom you anointed. They did what your power and will had decided beforehand should happen...." Of course, they were referring to Jesus' crucifixion. Then the chapter continues with a description, "After they prayed, the place where they were meeting was shaken. And they were all filled with the Holy Spirit and spoke the word of God boldly" (verse 31).

Mike then observes wryly, "I guess this passage shows us how to gain more courage to share God with others. We need the filling of the Spirit each day."

Bruce continues, "I agree. Notice that the church described the mystery of God's perfect plan. He used the sins of the religious leaders' jealousy and hatred of Jesus, similar to the sins of Joseph's brothers against him, to bring about Jesus' death in order to rescue us from our imperfections. God's plan to send his innocent, perfect Son to the cross included and overcame what I believe were the worst sins ever committed by humans, for which they were fully guilty!"

I comment with a frown, "It's hard to believe!"

Bruce responds, "I'll give you an example of the fact that God's plan and our human responsibility are both true. I learned that God wants me to pray for little things as well as big things when a woman coming from the opposite direction turned in front of me when I was going through a yellow light in Saskatoon, Saskatchewan, Canada, a city of 225,000, where we lived before we moved to South Dakota. That accident totaled my 1990 Maxima.

"I had always prayed for safety on our long trips, but that time I was just driving from the south side, where we lived next to our church, to the west side where I was going to visit members of our church. I didn't arrive there that night because of my accident. Later, I sensed that God's lesson for me from that experience was to pray about short trips and everything else too.

"Therefore, last year on the first day of ticket sales in February, I wanted to get Cubs tickets for the following summer during one of the cheaper games and prayed that God would bless my efforts, if he wanted us to go to that game. Well, on that first day of ticket sales at 9:30 A.M., a half-hour before the ticket sales started, I clicked the ticket button on the Cubs' web site to get into the 'Ticket Waiting Room.' I waited *five hours* there, while praying for God's blessing on my efforts, watching the monitor screen, and reading *The Reason for God* by Timothy Keller—a very good book, by the way.

"Well, finally I quit waiting in the waiting room, which I could also call the 'Futility Room.' Instead, I decided to imitate my successful plan to get a 1989 Cubs World Series non-ticket for a non-World-Series game by dialing and re-dialing over and over again on the phone. (By the way, I got my money back in 1989!)

"In this case, I pressed the ticket button on the Cubs schedule for the date I wanted every fifteen or thirty seconds over and over again, praying all the time and figuring that one of those times God would put me at the head of the waiting line in the 'Futility Room.' Wonder of wonders, I got into the Ticket Room after only seventeen minutes of repeated re-clicking at 3:17 P.M. It wasn't a 'Futility Room' after all! God's plan for me to get tickets finally kicked in after five hours and seventeen minutes, while I prayed and clicked, the persistence of which he also prompted and then blessed. God's plan and my effort worked together."

Mike then asks for prayer requests. As I fidget, I am the first one to share my desperate situation, and everyone sits in stunned silence until the group prays fervently for my healing in every way. In addition, we pray for God's grace to submit to his will, whatever it will be.

Then we all share tears and hugs as we part. During another meeting on the sidewalk in the front of Mike's duplex, Bruce, Holly, and I decide to go golfing the next day for the last time that season and possibly forever.

CHAPTER 63

Late golf

It was a cool, crisp day with a hint of the coming fall and winter with a little sharp edge to the moving air. Holly, Joe, and I again engaged in the human-versus-golf-course battle that they usually won and that I usually lost. However, that day Joe paid for us to use a golf cart that he rode between shots, and he played his shots weakly for the first four holes. However, he rode in the passenger's seat of the cart and watched Holly and me play during the last five holes.

We played in silence until, after we teed off on the third hole, Joe asked me with a muffled voice, "What do ya think happens immediately after we die, Bruce? I heard once that some people think that we sleep in death until we rise from the dead, if indeed that event will happen."

As Joe drove and Holly and I walked to our balls on and off the third fairway, I answered Joe's question, "Inspired Paul assumed that our souls immediately go to God for judgment and entrance into heaven or hell. There are two passages in which Paul writes about death. In Philippians one, he was facing possible death at his future trial before Emperor Nero. His and God's choice was between his remaining in his body for the benefit of other Christians or going to be with Christ in death. He amazingly wrote, 'To live is Christ and to die is gain.' In other words, both choices are God's blessings for believers. In 2 Corinthians 5, Paul's language also assumes that death will be a time of leaving his body like a tent folding up and of waiting for God's building, the resurrection body."

After we whacked our golf balls in the general direction of the third green, Joe shared his fear, "Bruce, I'm scared that when I die, I'll either stop existing or end up in hell, suffering more horribly than I am now!"

Holly shared, "Joe, God has assured me with his gift of the new birth that I will be with Jesus."

Holly and I walked to our golfballs as I observed, "I'm scared stiff that the latter destination is going to be yours, but there's still time for you to believe in Jesus as your Rescuer from hell for heaven. I believe that that's why God put Holly and me in your life—to rescue you!"

Holly remarked, "That's right, Bruce."

"Bruce," Joe suddenly remarked as he gently chipped his ball to within six inches of the third cup, "It would be great if we could play golf together in the new creation that you've talked about, but I still can't quite believe in your God."

I delivered a friendly shot back at him after I chipped out of the deep rough over the green into the bordering trees—par for my course!—"Well, if we do play golf there, we'll probably make a hole-in-one on every hole! We won't be bored at our success either.

"However, I know, Joe, that God's just plan to punish the sinful, self-centered rebellion of the human race is going to take place when Jesus returns. Either he will punish us for our rebellion against him or he will accept us because of our trust in Jesus' death as our substitute with the resulting surrender of our lives to his guidance. That choice has to be ours before we die."

As Joe uttered those dreaded words, "You're still out," I dropped my ball in play near the line of trees bordering the third green under "winter rules," which duffers play when it's to their benefit.

My answering shot was a holed chip from the rough, accompanied by my yelp, "Whoopee!"

Holly and Joe cheered too at my unbelievable shot, Holly made par, and Joe easily rolled in his short putt for a birdie. As we carted to the fourth tee, Joe said, "This is my last hole, Bruce. My body's telling me to sit out the rest of the holes. I'll drive you around the rest of the course."

As we teed off with straight, long drives, Joe confided in us, "I got the call this morning, Holly and Bruce. Mayo wants to do something called Whipple surgery on my pancreatic tumor along with radiation and chemo at about the same time to keep it from spreading any farther."

Holly asked, "Joe, when is your surgery?"

"It's two weeks from today."

I asserted, "Joe, I'm positive that God has arranged your life to bring eternal good out of all of your suffering for eternal life!"

Joe mumbled, "It's just that I still have trouble believing in an invisible God as my Father."

I sent a secret request to God and asked Joe, "Do you believe in the atom with its nucleus and electrons?"

He sat back in the electric golfcart as we rode to chase our little, dimpled, white balls, "Of course, that belief is a given."

"Well, then, how can you believe in the atom when no one has ever seen one?"

"Well, they've seen the light trail when the atom is split,...but *I* see your point! We can see God's actions and his plans by visible events because the Bible shows us the visible Jesus and his teachings and actions. That's your point, isn't it, Bruce?"

"Yeah, you've got it, my friend! I saw a TV program the other night about the atom. The design and regularity of the invisible atom in my mind points to an invisible divine Designer and our Father-Creator. However, humans are also responsible for how they use the atom. I'm afraid that they haven't used it very responsibly and will answer to God for their recklessness.

"Another example of God's plan and human responsibility is Paul's description of his 'thorn in the flesh,' which he doesn't explain further. It was some physical problem that he pleaded three times for God to take away. However, he said that God left it in his life as a 'messenger of Satan' to keep Paul humble. Then God said to Paul that his grace was sufficient for Paul to be able to live with it. Paul prayed, but it was up to God to take it away or not. However, God in his love will bring good out of every situation for all believers. I hope that you can make that leap of faith before you meet God."

On the sixth hole with a hill blocking our view of the hole, there was a pond on my right and several thin, widely-spaced trees with leaves only high at their tops. After I teed off, I yelped joyfully when my golf ball cleared the pond in the right direction. As I stood over my ball, my next shot made the satisfying thud that I seldom heard. The ball sailed in the general direction of the green. However, my satisfaction at my well-hit shot was short-lived. The ball hit one of those trees just to the right of center and flew with a loud clunk back into the pond that I had just escaped!

Joe and Holly yelled in unison, "O, no, Bruce!"

I yelled in return, "That shot was frustrating,...but really funny!" as a full smile creased my face. As I dropped another ball, we laughed for several minutes.

We finished the rest of the course with Joe observing my silly slices and horrendous hooks and Holly's straight shots. At the course's end on the ninth tee, we again marveled at the scenery dominated by the mighty Mississippi. As I drove Joe to his apartment building on Faith Street, I assured him again that I would pray extra-hard for him. However, I also said that God always knows best. I then deposited Holly at her apartment house.

* * *

> But Joseph said [to his brothers], "Don't be afraid. Am I in the place of God? You intended to harm me [by selling me into slavery], but God intended it for good to accomplish what is now being done, the saving of many lives [through Joseph's second-in-command rulership of Egypt]."
>
> (Genesis 50:19, 20)

Part Fourteen Questions:

1. With whom did God make the old covenant? With whom does God make the new covenant? Give an example of an old-covenant law and the way that it is followed under the new covenant.
2. What do you think about the narrator's definition of the covenant and the new form under which we live? How have you experienced that covenant relationship with God? Explain.
3. How does Joe gain insight into the difference and similarity between our present and future bodies? How are the difference and similarity like the new covenant? How eagerly do you look forward to the resurrection of your body? Why?
4. What did Jesus mean when he said that the wine was the blood of the new covenant? How does that blood affect your life today? Explain.
5. What progress do you see in Joe, spiritually? How can we gain spiritual progress?

PART 15

How does God overcome doubt permanently?

CHAPTER 64

Baptism

For the next two weeks of anxious waiting for Joe's surgery, Holly and I were saddened to see Joe doing fewer and fewer laps and then finally going to the hot-tub without swimming, too exhausted to swim at all. Trying to keep our minds off of Joe's condition, we continued our discussions about Christian beliefs. One day Joe entered the hot-tub with a very slow limp without swimming when I greeted him with my grinning comment, "So, Joe, you didn't want to be immersed today?"

"Whatcha say?"

"You know. Ya didn't want to be immersed, sprinkled, baptized?"

"O, no—no baptism for Joe today. By the way, that baptism at your church on Sunday was interesting. I noticed references to the new birth and the covenant that we've been talking about. Do you believe that God—if he does exist—did his thing with the baby when the water was sprinkled on her in the name of the 3-in-1 God?"

"Incidently, Joe, did ya notice that it was the '*name*' (singular) of the 3-in-1 God that the pastor used to baptize the baby?" Joe nodded as I continued, "No, I don't believe that the water has any special divine power to give the baby the new birth at the time of that ceremony. We believe that baptism is, instead, God's welcome of the baby into the covenant community. It also involves the parents' promises to raise the child to believe in that God. Those actions are the two parts of the covenant. Whereas the old covenant had circumcision to welcome a baby into the Israelite community of God, the new covenant points to the new birth with public baptism. Holly, what do you believe now?

Holly replied, "The Catholic church believes that there are seven sacraments, one of which is the baptism of babies. There is an urgency for them to baptize babies as soon as possible after birth. That quickness to baptize happens because they believe that after the priest blesses the water, it becomes holy water that gives the baby the Triune God's special grace. However, I don't find that teaching in the Bible and tend to agree with you now."

My reply was immediate, "If the Christian Reformed Church believed that the baptismal water gives God's gift of the new birth, I wouldn't be a CRC member today, since God gave me the new birth without outward baptism as I attended a Baptist church. I had already been baptized both as a baby and as a 12-year-old. The Baptists taught that the baptism of adults was only a symbol of the new birth that has already taken place. In contrast, our church believes that God is present in the baptismal ceremony and in the family's future to bless the parents' responsibility to point their child to Jesus as they carry out their promises with their actions and words. Also, it's the child's responsibility to believe in God as he or she grows up."

Joe jumped in to ask, "Why can't Christians agree on something like baptism?"

I diffused Joe's friendly attack with my soft-spoken reply, "We may interpret the Bible somewhat differently, Joe, on what happens during baptism, depending on our cultures. However, all Christians firmly agree on the much more important beliefs that God is the 3-in-1 God and that the gift of the new birth from God is necessary for believers to trust in him and to turn away from their many imperfections. Furthermore, we all agree that baptism has replaced circumcision; that he is the one only true God, who acts in our lives; and that baptism points to the new birth.

"We *merely* don't agree on *when* the new birth happens: the Baptists, *before*...; the Catholics, *during*...; Reformed people, Methodists, and a large number of Lutherans, *after*...public baptism. That difference is *very* minor compared to the much-more-important beliefs on which we *do* agree."

Joe replied, "I...guess...you're right." Holly high-fived me, as we splashed water in all directions.

My next question was directed at our friend Joe, "How are ya doing, Joe—really?"

He replied after a long sigh, "I'm hanging in there. I just wish my surgery were here and done. It's another week and a day of waiting!"

My pursuit of Joe's feelings continued, "That *does* seem like a long time. How are you *feeling*?"

Joe sensed my urgent concern with his forlorn answer, "Scared....I just wish that I had the faith in God that both of you have."

Holly answered Joe's wish with her confidence, "I think that you will have it sometime."

I nodded my agreement and changed the subject, "Joe, I've been curious about something. You don't swear or use any crude language. How did your clean language come about?"

Joe straightened up from his usual slump, "Well, one time my father was out in his garage tinkering around when I was seven or eight years old. When he suddenly hammered his thumb hard instead of a nail, he let out a cloud of profanity that would even embarrass prisoners in a prison. I was playing in the garage at the time with my toy tractors, and I felt bad for my father. At some point I decided never to say those or other crude words again."

I chimed in with a chuckle, "A similar event happened in my life. On one especially hot day, all of the guys in our family were crankily bringing in the hay, my least favorite job on the farm besides forking manure!" Holly and Joe smirked at my comment as I continued, "The hay elevator that carried the bails to the second-floor hayloft of our flat-roofed barn suddenly broke down! (I must have been about twelve years old.) My unbelieving dad, who never swore in my presence that I can remember, let out a string of expletives that would curl your hair, if it weren't already curly!

"Well, even though I wasn't a believer yet, I was extremely embarrassed for Dad and resolved never to say such words again. It seems to me, Joe, that God was already working with both of us those times as parts of his plan, even though neither one of us was a believer!"

Both Joe and I shared grins while Holly said, "I was taught that those words are wrong and dishonoring to God!" Then she suddenly grinned her big, beautiful smile and exclaimed, "*Hey*, we all agree on something!" We all high-fived so much that more water seemed to end up outside the hot-tub than inside it.

I ventured, "Joe and Holly, I've also noticed that you don't use the word 'like' much, unlike a lot of young adults. I'm curious why that is."

Holly answered, "My English teacher in tenth grade categorically told us that using the word 'like' as anything other than a preposition with an object was wrong. The kids didn't especially like her, but I decided to avoid too many 'likes' in my speech."

Joe chimed in, "Yeah, I also had 'Old Lady,' I mean, Mrs. Miller and stopped using 'like' too much because of her command."

CHAPTER 65

Fervent prayer

It was the end of September when our Bible-discussion-prayer-support group met in a special meeting to pray for Joe's surgery. A volunteer first read Psalm 139, David's amazing description about God's total knowledge of us and his everywhere-present nature, and opened with prayer. George, at whose house we met, started the discussion with a typical group-facilitator's question, "Which verses especially impress you?"

Joe responded with a deadly seriousness that I had seldom seen, "You mean God—if he does exist as the Creator of each one of us from conception on—is also everywhere?!"

I spoke up, "Yes, he was even in the *womb* with us after creating us there. Now you can see why so many of us are opposed to selfish, senseless abortions!"

Larry, usually our group comic, spoke up with a furrowed forehead, "Yeah, fifty million abortions since *Roe versus Wade* have added up to a national tragedy!" We all nodded.

I shared with the group my experience, "This psalm comforts me because of my time in my mother's womb when my three-year-old brother, Bobby, was sick with leukemia. Verse 13 is really important to me: 'For you created my inmost being; you knit me together in my mother's womb.' I'm sure that my parents were under a lot of pressure at that time. Bobby died two and a half months after I was born. God has been with me powerfully all these years in spite of the fact that that experience in the womb and during my early months made me very sensitive to stress."

Joe exclaimed, "Will the amazing things in your life never end?!"

I showed my widest smile, "No, Joe, they won't, since I'm confident that God has given me eternal life out of his pure grace. Therefore, I believe that his amazing events in my life will *never* end!" We all had a hearty laugh together, which served as a needed stress reliever.

At our share-and-prayer time we stormed God's throne room with our submissive, yet bold prayers for Joe's successful surgery. George closed those prayers, "Dear almighty God, we implore you for your healing power in Joe's life and for whatever he needs. Guide the surgeon's hands day after tomorrow to overcome the cancer in his body, according to your sovereign will described in Psalm 139. And yet we put Joe in your merciful, loving hands. You know best. Through Jesus, who conquered many diseases and death for people during his life on earth, we pray that you will heal Joe in every way. Yet we submit to your perfect will. Amen!" All of us echoed his "amen" fervently and ended our time together with heartfelt hugs and more than a few tears.

The next day Joe and his sister drove to Rochester north of the Minnesota stateline so that the capable medical staff at Mayo Clinic could prepare Joe for his serious surgery. Our group's individual prayers continued to accompany him into surgery, where he was in the divine Surgeon's hands.

CHAPTER 66

First visit

Four days after Joe's surgery, Phyllis drove him to the rehab wing in our local New Life Nursing Home. I drove over to the other side of town to visit him there. I found him but hardly recognized him in an electric wheelchair, since his emaciated body looked almost as old as many of the other residents there. As I entered his light-and-cheery room with a southern exposure, the sunlight flooding the room contrasted with Joe's weakened condition. Joe greeted me with as much of a joyful squeak as he could muster, "Hi, Bruce! How are ya doin'?"

"I'm doin' OK. How are *you* doin', Joe?" I managed to spit out inspite of myself.

Joe said with a slight gleam in his eyes, "I'm doin' *lo-uh-ve-ly*!"

My measured reply shifted our conversational gears to seriousness, "How did the surgery go? What did they find?"

Joe matched the gravity of my inquiry with his barely-audible answer, "Well, they got the tumor and patched up my pancreas and vessels. However, Bruce, they found cancer several other places." His voice trailed off at the end of his sad announcement.

I sat down on a folding chair in shock and blurted out my response, "O no, Joe, that's awful!" as a tear traced its mournful journey down my left cheek.

We sat a long time in Joe's cheery, sunny room in the valley of the shadow of death without speaking until Joe slowly said, "Bruce, I've actually started praying to God—if he's there—for faith."

"That's great, Joe! I'm sure that God will answer you!"

A thirty-something, heavy-set nurse entered Joe's room to give him his meds when he said, "I'm in a lot of pain. These meds only take off a little of its edge. Now I know a little of your struggle with pain over the years, Bruce."

"I hope that you can get more relief than you've gotten so far. Is there anything you want me to do?"

"Could ya stay a little while longer with me, Bruce?"

With my ready agreement, Joe and I sat a long time in his room with a sleeping, older man named Pete in the other half of his sunny and cheery, dark and dreary room without saying much but experiencing God's presence.

CHAPTER 67

An amazing visit

One week later I visited Joe a second time at New Life. That time I found him in his wheelchair next to the nurses' station facing the entrance and writhing forward and backward with severe pain. I sat on a folding chair knee-to-knee with him and asked him urgently if he would like me to pray with him. After his surprising, nodded consent, I prayed simply and quietly, "Father, we pray through Jesus in the Spirit that you will come into Joe's life and ease his pain. Through Jesus alone we pray, amen!"

Joe suddenly grasped my old-because-of-age hands with his old-before-their-time hands in a vice grip and exclaimed with bugged-out eyes, "Bruce, there's power coming from you!"

I instantly knew what was happening and answered him, "That's Jesus' divine power, Joe!" Then Joe slumped backward, seemingly relieved of his pain.

I left him with a thankful heart, while praising God for his great power, as I drove to our condo.

* * *

I enter Joe's room to see him lying flat with no energy even to raise himself up. *I'm very sad to see this guy that I've grown to love looking so fragile and old.*

Joe greets me with a squeak, "Hi, Holly! I'm glad that you came. Guess what happened to me. Bruce visited me, and Jesus entered my life! Bruce prayed for me, and I felt power that God sent through him to me! Now, I'm a changed person believing in the 3-in-1 God that I was skeptical about for so long."

"That's wonderful, Joe! Now, Jesus has given both of us the new birth."

"Yeah, it's great to have faith in Bruce's God as my God and yours."

"How are you doing physically, Joe?"

"Not so hot, but I now have hope for that resurrection body that Bruce has talked about." *It's really hard for me to see Joe so weak, but I'm thankful that God has changed him.*

A tear streaks its way down my cheek as I say, "Joe, I hate seeing you this way. I love you."

"I love you too, Holly. We'll see each other again sometime."

"Don't talk that way, Joe. Maybe you'll recover from this severe sickness."

"I doubt that that change will happen, Holly."

"There you are doubting again." We smile at Joe's doubts.

O, God, I pray for Joe's recovery. Jesus healed many people. You can heal his wide-spread cancer even now. Help me to accept your answer if it is "no."

CHAPTER 68

An exciting visit

A week after my last visit, I returned to find Joe in his room. He lay flat with very little strength. As I stood above him, I asked, "Joe, what happened to you last week?"

With a raspy, unfamiliar voice, he squeaked eagerly with all the energy that he could muster, while rambling haltingly but excitedly, "Bruce, *Jesus* came into my life!...*Your* 3-in-1 God is now *my* 3-in-1 God!...Jesus is my Road to travel to my new, perfect Father in heaven by the Spirit's work!...He answered my prayers for faith!...His power is unbelievable!...He has changed my life to believe in him and turn away from my lifelong, sinful skepticism and many imperfections which had previously controlled me!" Though Joe was extremely weak, his newly-found, God-given ecstasy was contagious.

"That's fantastic, Joe! I'm excited that God used me, but *he* was the one who changed you, Joe!"

"Yeah, I know, Bruce. Would you read Psalm 23? It's going through my head."

I read that comforting passage, and we rejoiced together that the 3-in-1 God was now Joe's good Shepherd. I also read Psalm 66, a psalm of praise for God's answers to prayer. I then prayed with Joe in mutual faith, "Thank you, all-powerful God—Father, Jesus, and Holy Spirit, one ever-living God—for coming into Joe's life! We praise you that you gave him the new birth last week by the baptism of the Holy Spirit and that you gave him your forgiveness for his rebellion and doubts. Through Jesus, Joe's Rescuer, we honor you, amen." Joe replied weakly but joyfully, "Amen!"

I then sat with Joe for a long time as we basked in the greatness of God's glow on a cloudy day.

When I left Joe's bedside, I floated through the hallway up somewhere near cloud twelve as I thought about Joe's amazing conversion. I stopped at the nurse's station near the entrance to ask about Joe's condition. An older, gray-haired nurse answered my inquiry, "He's extremely weak, but he's been telling everyone the experience that he and you had last week. I saw you here that time, but I had no idea that God was working in such a powerful way between you two! Many of us are praising God for his amazing work."

All I could manage with a wide grin, out of my whirlpool of emotions, was an exclamation, "That's great! I praise the God of all believers, including Joe!" I drove home with a great number of emotions swirling through my consciousness, the strongest of which was thankful joy.

When I arrived home, Winnie rejoiced with me about Joe's experience. At supper and before bedtime, we lifted up our all-powerful God in prayer and praise for his life-changing strength.

Three days later, before I planned to visit Joe again, our telephone rang.

CHAPTER 69

A tragic triumph

Joe's sister, Phyllis, shared with me on the phone the sad news that Joe had died a short time before her call.

The Smith family did not know any other minister as well as they knew me. As a result, I consented to their request to lead Joe's memorial service with a mixture of both reluctance because Joe was my dear friend and eagerness to share with grieving people God's good news along with Joe's last experiences.

The Smith family decided to have Joe's remains cremated and buried before the service. I had shared with them my preference for having a casket or an urn present during the service as an object lesson of the reality of death so that the mourners could face death visually. However, they felt that with the high costs of burials nowadays, they would prefer to have his body cremated and buried before the service. I reluctantly agreed, because the family always has the final say in such matters.

The organ was already playing when I arrived and led the family in prayer in another room. Then we all slowly walked into the chapel, the front of which was full of flowers. The result was that there was little room for the tiny podium dwarfed by my large frame. I began the service with some Bible passages about Jesus' resurrection and the resurrection of the body at Jesus' return along with a few short prayers.

Then a few mourners, including Holly, spoke haltingly and movingly about Joe as a fun-loving, shining light in their lives. George also spoke, "Joe's skepticism about God gave me a few doubts and drove me to study the Bible again for its convincing evidence that the Triune God came in Jesus to save us. That study, prompted by Joe's doubts, strengthened my faith in the God of the Bible and increased my hope for Jesus' Second Coming."

My message was entitled "A Tragic Triumph." I began it by summarizing the years that Joe and I spent discussing Christian beliefs at the local indoor swimming pool. I also summarized Joe's doubts and my testimonies about God's existence and work in my life. I am convinced that I was able to continue speaking with God's leading and strength inspite of my grief, "Joe was too young to die at almost thirty-nine years old! But we will *all* die. We will all be cremated or settle into a grave. But the question arises, what happens *after* we die? I believe the Bible's truth that we will all then appear before God, our Creator and Judge.

"Furthermore, the fact is that Jesus said, 'Be perfect, as your Father in heaven is perfect.' And *not one* of us is perfect! No one would even claim to be. As a result, how can we *imperfect* people—made by a perfect God, the only true, 3-in-1 God—enter his perfect place to live with him? We can't make our imperfect lives perfect again. We certainly can't earn heaven by any of our imperfect actions.

"*However*, God provided the answer to the problem of our imperfection by sending Jesus, the only perfect Person—the God-man—who died as a perfect substitute in our place. The result is that all humans who trust in Jesus, who rose from the dead, as the only way to God the Father may be *made* perfect in God's sight *now* and *perfect* in *every* way when we die, the state in which I'm assured that Joe is now. God's rescue happens with what the Bible describes as the new birth, to which water baptism points.

"Joe never received that ceremony. However, like the believing criminal next to Jesus on the cross, I'm positive that he has gone to be with Jesus. How can I be so sure about his destination beyond death? In doubting, skeptical Joe's case, he had been attending one of our church's Bible-discussion groups as well as our church. However, mere attendance at church does not make a person perfect in God's sight, nor does trying to be a good person in our own strength ensure our entrance into heaven.

"Only a personal trust in the God-man Jesus gets us God's approval and our final perfection with him. It does not come from some outward ceremony like baptism or attendance at church, which are, however, important for believers' progress in Christian living.

"The reason that I'm sure about Joe's destination is an amazing event that happened when I came to visit Joe at the New Life Nursing Home for the second time. There, I found him sitting in his electric wheelchair near the nurses' station. I found a folding chair and sat facing him knee-to-knee. I asked him as he writhed forward and backward in strong pain if he wanted me to pray for him. He nodded in painful agony. I then said a short prayer asking God to enter Joe's life and relieve his pain.

"Then, Joe opened his eyes wide, straightened up, grabbed my hands tightly with his hands, and exclaimed with all of his limited strength, 'Bruce, there's power coming from you!' I knew immediately what was happening and replied excitedly, 'Joe, that's Jesus' divine power!' Joe then relaxed, seemingly with less pain.

"The next time I saw Joe and asked him what had happened to him on my previous visit, he said with all the excitement that he could muster in his severely-weakened state, 'Jesus came into my life! Your 3-in-1 God is now my 3-in-1 God, and I now have a perfect heavenly Father!' and accepted eagerly my reading of two passages from the Bible and my prayer.

"*Doubting* Joe had become *believing* Joe because he had received God's gift of the new birth, faith, and the ability to turn away from his sinful skepticism—all by way of Jesus' life, death, and resurrection! I'm convinced, because of that unusual, true experience, that when Joe died *tragically*—he was way too young to die!—he instead experienced, after death, the *triumph* of God's approval as well as perfection in heaven!

"All of us who believe in Jesus' life, death, and resurrection as the way to God the Father's acceptance receive both his free approval (that is, grace) in the present that changes our lives along with the new birth as well as final perfection beyond the grave. In the same way, I'm completely assured that believing Joe, at the end of and now beyond his short life, has experienced those blessings. It is my prayer that all of us can experience a personal relationship with Jesus that will carry us on angels' wings into the next life and to our future resurrection to join Joe and Jesus. Amen!"

I followed my message with a short prayer and the memorial service with God's parting blessing from 1 Corinthians 13:14, which is Paul's blessing from the Triune God, "May the grace of the Lord Jesus Christ, the love of God, and the fellowship of the Holy Spirit be with all of you. Amen." As the memorial-service attenders filed out and while most of them averted their gaze from mine, the organist played slowly the song that fit a service dedicated to the one, only true God, who provided skeptic-turned-believer Joe Smith with his "Amazing Grace."

During the lunch in our church following the memorial service, I stopped at the table of Joe's family on my way to the food line and asked them, "Would you want me to drop by to visit with you about Joe?"

Phil spoke promptly, "You can come as a friend, Bruce, but not as a pastor. We have our memories of Joe's life."

Since the Smith family's table was full, I sat at a table with Holly and other members of our small group, who all warmly expressed their appreciation for my remarks during the service. I responded, "Thank you. I feel that God blessed me with those words about his Word."

Holly quoted Joe with a smile, while using his comical, nasal, Gomer Pyle-like voice, "Well-said, preacher-man! I'll see you in church Sunday." We all laughed in the Spirit of Joe's joy in Jesus.

* * *

Dear friends, now we are children of God, and what we will be has not been made known. But we know that when Christ appears, we shall be like him, for we shall see him as he is. All who have this hope in him purify themselves, just as he is pure.

(1 John 3:2,3)

* * *

Part Fifteen Questions:

1. Why is the word "cancer" so scary? How can we face such suffering that may come to us? Referring to Paul's "thorn in the flesh," how can this reference help your faith? 2. What do you think about the discussion group's responses to Joe's sickness?
3. How do you respond to the narrator and Joe's discussion at the golf course about death? Why do we tend to put the idea of death out of our minds? How does that discussion help your faith? Or does it increase your doubts? Why?
4. What do you know about our life after death? What will the two possible destinations be like? Where are you going after you die? How do you know?
5. How does the narrator's misadventure with the tall, thin trees and the pond strike you compared with the seriousness of the rest of this section?
6. How have your reading and/or discussion of this book affected your life? Explain.

CPSIA information can be obtained at www.ICGtesting.com
Printed in the USA
LVOW042037120612

285855LV00001B/6/P